AWAKEN

First Print Edition: 2025
Printed in the United States of America

For a full list of recommended books and resources, scan the QR code below:

Check out the
Shop tab

AWAKEN

I SUFFERED. I LEARNED. I CHANGED.

BY AISA MARIE MAGSOMBOL

Published by Aisa Marie Writes,
an imprint of The Grassdoor & Co. LLC

TABLE OF CONTENTS

DEDICATIONS

First and foremost, to my daughter Charlotte: my greatest blessing, accomplishment, and supporter. I appreciate your patience, understanding, and continued encouragement as I have committed to sharing my story with the world. I love you forever, I like you for always, as long as I'm living, my Bebe you'll be.

To my other half, Michael, thank you for holding a space for me to discover healing and love, especially during some of my most difficult seasons. I am thankful for your full-spectrum creamer, which saved my life and I'm incredibly grateful for your timing, friendship, and partnership. You have inspired me to fulfill the potential I never desired before, and you persist in challenging me in all areas of my life. I love and appreciate you. Thank you for creating spaces and experiences with me.

Thank you to Christi, my best friend of 20+ years and Sister in Christ. I would never be brave enough to use my voice in the way God planned if it wasn't for you. Thank you for your wisdom, for consulting with me about all areas of life, and for encouraging me to write and share my story.

Lastly, my dear readers, this is my love letter to you: a friendly reminder that you are "Fearfully and wonderfully made" (Psalm 139:14 KJV) and to "Trust in the Lord with all your heart, and do not depend on your understanding." (Proverbs 3:5 NLT)

INTRODUCTION

Have you ever felt the weight of adversity and loneliness clinging to your heart like an unwelcome companion? Wondered if love, success, or happiness were truly meant for you? In the chaos of life, with constant distractions pulling you in every direction, have you ever felt lost, stuck or hopeless, searching for peace? If so, know this—you are not alone. As you read through *Awaken: I Suffered. I Learned. I Changed.*, remember that hope is real and triumph is within your reach.

My journey is one of survival to revival—but more importantly, it's about renewal. Every word in this book reflects my battles and victories; written so you might find your own story woven into mine.

In these honest reflections, you'll witness moments when life knocked me down—and my determination to rise, stronger and more resilient each time.

Awaken is more than a memoir—it's a transformation. Darkness into light, self-doubt into self-acceptance, pain into healing. It is a testament to the strength of the human spirit, the beauty of resilience, and the power of faith. Above all, it is a reminder that you possess the strength to heal no matter how deep your wounds are.

There may be times when the weight of my pain might feel tangible. In those moments, let it reflect your own struggles. Feel the rawness of each setback and experience the relief when the fog starts to lift. As I uncover the importance of spirituality, support systems, and self-reflection, I hope you will find inspiration to seek your own path toward healing and wholeness.

This is not just my story—it's a mirror for your own power. Whether through faith, inner strength, or the quiet resolve deep within you; you, too, can rise. And when you do, that light—your light—will guide you toward a life filled with purpose and fulfillment.

Allow my journey to awaken your spirit, touch your heart, and leave an unforgettable impression on your soul. Prepare to be moved, uplifted, and transformed. Together, we will walk the road of self-discovery. As we explore these pages, remember: you are worthy, fearfully and wonderfully made, and never alone. Your moment of awakening awaits.

CHAPTER ONE

FROM DARKNESS TO LIGHT

I can't do this anymore," he said.

A wave of disbelief hit me. My heart raced and I could feel my blood pressure rising, tension building in every muscle of my body.

"You can't do what?!" I replied, trying to keep my voice steady, though anger and confusion threatened to take over.

"This," he said. As if that one word could sum up the unraveling of our entire life together.

And just like that, with no real explanation, he was leaving me and our two-year-old daughter.

"I don't love you. I never loved you. You were nothing but a good fuck."

It was around November 2010, in between our birthdays. I felt like I was having a quarter-life crisis, and so was he. There had been so much tension and fighting between us. Anthony was turning 26 and in a darker place than I was. He was depressed, unemployed, and sinking deeper into his alcoholism.

He had gotten a DUI a few months earlier on his way home from the bar where he worked. That job didn't last long—he was fired for drinking while working. I couldn't wrap my head around it. I was busting my ass at work, trying to make things better for us while he was sabotaging everything.

I had left my job at Verizon Wireless because the hours at the bank were more accommodating, and the pay was better. I was positioning myself for a promotion—for our family. Meanwhile, my baby daddy thought nothing was wrong with drinking on the job because it was Monday Night Football at Buffalo Wild Wings, so why not?

I struggled so much during that time. I remember calling Water of Life Community Church—even though I was Catholic then—seeking some kind of Godly advice. I felt so torn. Should I stay with him and support him through his alcoholism? Or should I leave because I had one child to care for, and it wasn't him? I continued to fight for us, for our family.

I decided to move us to Perris, CA, which was more affordable than Rancho Cucamonga and closer to the Wells Fargo branch in Riverside, where I was working. I was doing everything I could to set our family up for success, and he was the one who said he couldn't do this anymore. It was just Charlotte and me at my family's party by Christmas time. I didn't tell them what had happened until the following year, though. I needed time and space to grieve.

When Anthony left, I felt broken—completely shattered. I was numb and scarcely remember how I managed at work during that time. There was no discussion about how we would move forward or what would happen with our daughter. He just left. He moved back in with his mom, and that was that.

Thankfully, Anthony's stepdad, Mike, didn't hesitate to offer Charlotte and me a place to stay with him and his girlfriend, Letty, in Norwalk. I have several Michael's in my life. All have played an influential role, mostly good, some bad.

This particular Mike was like a second father to me. He reminded me of Joseph (Jesus' stepdad) in the Bible— someone who loved unconditionally, even though we weren't related by blood. Both Anthony and Charlotte carry his last name, and that, especially, makes me happy. Mike had even cosigned on a loan with me when Anthony needed a car. But despite Mike and Letty's kindness, I couldn't stay long. The commute from Norwalk to Riverside was brutal, and the emotional toll was overwhelming.

I was sad, broken, angry, and lost; and it was colder there than I was used to. As much as I appreciated Mike and Letty's warm welcome, I decided to move back to my parent's house. Months later, Anthony and I celebrated Charlotte's third birthday at Disneyland but didn't discuss our situation. I was still angry, still heartbroken. His reasons for leaving? All bullshit. His cowardice, his refusal to be honest and mature, infuriated me.

I remember that night so clearly. Lying in bed after putting Charlotte to sleep, I couldn't hold back the tears anymore. I tossed and turned, and finally, I broke down. I wept.

God, why? What did I do to deserve this? Why is my family broken? Why am I following my mom's footsteps as much as I try not to? Why did he leave me? Why does everyone leave me?

I felt abandoned, not just by Anthony, but by life itself. *Should I have been nicer to him and his mom? Should I have submitted more to Anthony?* The guilt and confusion were suffocating.

And then, I finally hit my knees on my bedroom floor at my mom's house, making the ugly Kim K. cry—surrendering everything. That's when I heard it. A voice so clear that said, "I knew you wouldn't leave him, so I had him leave you."

At first, I was shocked. I didn't understand. *What do you mean, God? I wouldn't have left him, so you had to make him leave me?*

There was only silence—no further explanation. But something shifted in me. Although I was angry and scared of the unknown, something about that message was profound. It wasn't an immediate sense of peace, but over time, I realized that God was showing me that Anthony was not for me—that my daughter and I deserved better. It was a hard truth to accept, but it was the truth nonetheless.

God was teaching me to trust Him even when I couldn't see past the failure, the heartbreak, and the lack of answers; even when I felt like I had nothing left.

A few days later, on Good Friday in 2011, a childhood friend named Kristina invited me to worship at Water of Life Church. Several friends and coworkers had invited me to worship services before; Christian, Catholic, and Mormon, but I always turned them down, saying I was good. "I have a relationship with God, we're solid, and I don't need saving." Or so I thought.

But when Kristina invited me, the timing felt right. I don't know if it was because of the church or because I had already reached out to them prior, but I decided to go. That service was transformational. The church lights were dimmed as they played an audio testimony from a woman who had experienced an abortion and felt the weight of shame, only to discover God's grace. I tried to hold back, but I cried uncontrollably. Something broke in me that day, and that was that; I've been attending Water of Life ever since. Thank you, Lord, and for Kristina, too.

I have traveled a long and challenging road from darkness to light. Along the way, I've encountered both triumphs and trials that have shaped me into who I am today. As a single mother raising a teenager, I've faced the immense challenge of working full-time while striving to be present in every aspect of my daughter's life. From gymnastics and cheerleading to cooking classes, Girl Scouts, dance, acting, serving at church, and eventually homeschooling, pre-covid, I've prioritized staying deeply involved. It hasn't always been easy—far from it—but with love and determination, I've proven that being a devoted, successful single mother and pursuing my dreams can go hand in hand.

Life has thrown more curveballs than I can count. From childhood trauma and seeking love in all the wrong places to college changes and career moves; finding and losing myself multiple times along the way. Countless setbacks, each twist, and turn, have led me here—an accomplished entrepreneur, fully aware of who I am. I'm living a life filled with passion, purpose, and fulfillment. Through it all, I refuse to be defined by my circumstances or my past. Instead, I embrace every part of my journey and use those experiences to inspire others facing similar struggles.

As a Career & Life Coach and Author, my mission is to empower individuals to rise above adversity, discover their true identity, and create a life filled with purpose and fulfillment. My transformation has taught me the importance of perseverance, self-discovery, and answering the call of our true purpose. I hope to pass these lessons on to you, dear reader, so you, too, can unlock your full potential and create the life you deserve.

Let's embark on this journey together. Let's embrace our stories, overcome challenges, and step into the light waiting for us.

"YOU ARE THE LIGHT THAT
SHINES FOR THE WORLD TO SEE.
YOU ARE LIKE A CITY BUILT ON A
HILL THAT CANNOT BE HIDDEN."

MATTHEW 5:14 ERV

AWAKEN & *Reflect*

Take a moment to explore these questions with honesty and grace. There are no right or wrong answers—only your journey unfolding.

AWARENESS:

When have I experienced a moment of darkness that led to a deeper understanding of myself or my faith?

_____

_____

_____

_____

_____

_____

_____

_____

_____

_____

_____

_____

_____

_____

_____

_____

_____

_____

WORK IT:

What helped me take the first step toward healing,
even when it felt impossible?

_____

_____

_____

_____

_____

_____

_____

_____

_____

_____

_____

_____

_____

_____

_____

_____

_____

_____

ALIGNMENT:

Who or what has been a source of light for me in difficult times?

_____

_____

_____

_____

_____

_____

_____

_____

_____

_____

_____

_____

_____

_____

_____

_____

_____

_____

_____

_____

_____

KNOWLEDGE:

What lessons have I gained from
past struggles that now guide me?

_____

_____

_____

_____

_____

_____

_____

_____

_____

_____

_____

_____

_____

_____

_____

_____

_____

_____

EMBRACE:

How can I remind myself that God's presence
is with me, even in challenging moments?

_____

_____

_____

_____

_____

_____

_____

_____

_____

_____

_____

_____

_____

_____

_____

_____

_____

_____

_____

_____

NAVIGATE:

What is one way I can be a light
for myself or others today?

_____

_____

_____

_____

_____

_____

_____

_____

_____

_____

_____

_____

_____

_____

_____

"THE LIGHT SHINES IN THE DARKNESS, AND THE
DARKNESS HAS NOT OVERCOME IT."
– JOHN 1:5

CHAPTER TWO

FRAGMENTS OF THE PAST

It didn't necessarily feel like it at the time. Still, as I got older, I gradually became aware that my childhood was marked by what seemed like an ongoing series of abandonment, neglect, and feelings of rejection, leaving unforgettable scars on my young mind and tender spirit. As I contemplate my early years, I recall the absence of my biological father, a figure whom I grew up resenting as he went ghost before I could even comprehend his significance. My father was out of my life before I was two years old. I often looked at my old baby albums in confusion as to why this man would put effort into creating memories and decorating an album, only to disappear.

When I started school, it was a little embarrassing; I hadn't realized it then, but I knew that other kids either had two parents or divorced parents. Divorced parents almost seemed like the norm then. No one I knew had an absent father like me, though. I grew up pondering "What if" questions from time to time, but thankfully, I had my

Uncle Michael and stepdad (whom I affectionately refer to as "Baba"). I didn't need that other guy, nor did I have a desire to seek him out.

Fast forward to the summer of 2005, my Big Bro from Beta Upsilon Delta told me my sister messaged him on AOL Instant Messenger to contact me. I replied to Derrick, "Um, I have a little brother, not a sister." And that's when the curtain lifted on the soap opera that is my life.

Long story short, my dad was already married when he married my mom. He had two daughters from his first marriage, then married my mom in 1983. That same year, another sister was conceived with a third woman. I was born in 1985 and in 1986, my father had another daughter with his first wife. We also have a brother that I haven't met yet. I know of six siblings and four different mothers. This isn't just family drama—it's straight out of a [Filipino] telenovela!

Despite meeting and getting to know my sisters, a few cousins, and discovering the truth about my dad's lies and infidelity, my dad continued to deny who I was or that I even existed. We finally met a few years later, along with his first wife. She was pleasant. But that's enough about that for now.

——————— • • • ———————

My mom, overwhelmed by the pain and anger of the abandonment, would hold me tightly, her tears mingling with whispered rants of how my dad had another family and had left us. Even before uncovering this tangled web of lies, abandonment had already defined my childhood. That sense of feeling discarded for someone else became one of the earliest imprints on my little soul.

It was 1989, and we were the first in our family to move

out of the Los Angeles area. Before I started kindergarten, we relocated to Fontana, where I lived with my grandmother, whom I called Mama, along with my aunt, who I refer to as my Ate Joy, and my Uncle Michael, the youngest of my mom's siblings. They were still teenagers then, but they brought a sense of comfort and stability to my otherwise chaotic world.

My mother's presence, however, remained elusive, fading away like a distant memory. Although she had bought the house we all lived in, she continued to stay in Los Angeles, working at various hospitals and living at our old Arlington house with one of my uncles. Even though I knew why she was away, it didn't stop the feeling of being left behind. The details of those years are vague now, blurred by time and distance.

What I do vividly remember is the overwhelming sense of abandonment that washed over me when I started school, hitting me in waves that came and went until I reached first grade. I cried hysterically every morning, hyperventilating and unable to calm down. I believed I wasn't adequately socialized then because I never attended preschool. But in adulthood, I realized that these early days were the beginning of my separation anxiety and perhaps panic attacks. Each day my mom left, I'd clutch at her legs, convinced she might never return. That was the ache of my delicate spirit—the fear that, just like my father, my mother, too, would leave me behind.

My mom married my stepdad when I was eight years old, which significantly affected my life. The concept of having a father figure was new to me, and our family dynamics were unfamiliar. My mom and I barely had a relationship ourselves, which only added to my confusion and discomfort. They continued to live in Los Angeles. Meanwhile, I was in Fontana. Fortunately, the birth of my younger brother, Giovanni, soon after was a source of immense joy and excitement. I channeled all the love I yearned for into him, trying to fill the void within myself and feeling comfort in knowing I wasn't alone anymore.

Questions unsettled my mind, my thoughts like an unrelenting storm. *Why did my mother leave me to navigate life on my own? Was abandonment my fate? Like my absent father, now my mother? Was Mama going to leave me, too?*

The changes didn't stop there. Baba, who is Lebanese, was trying to raise his new Filipino-American stepdaughter, and it brought its own set of challenges—cultural differences that led to misunderstandings, arguments, and constant tension. Additionally, my mom made little effort to ensure a smooth and loving transition for everyone. Many life-changing moments occurred to me and around me, but there was little to no direct discussion with me. I was caught in a whirlwind of change without understanding how to comprehend it all.

And just when I began navigating this new reality, another change hit hard. Mama, who had been my rock, my constant, and the one who raised me since I was a baby, suddenly decided to remarry and move out. Mama wasn't just my grandmother; she was my everything. Mama walked me to and from school, chaperoned my field trips, and taught me how to care for myself, the dogs, and the house. We spent mornings watching *The Price is Right*, afternoons watching *All My Children* and *General Hospital* (I wasn't a fan of *One Life to Live*), and ending the day with *Monday Night Raw* wrestling or a Lakers game. She showed me how to shop garage sale deals on a Saturday morning and even taught me how to cook just enough to survive—basic meals, but they carried the weight of her love and care.

When Mama moved out abruptly, it shattered my sense of home and security. The family tension surrounding her new husband and her new living situation was too complex for me to fully understand at such a young age, but the emotional burden was undeniable. I was hurt and angry, perhaps a little resentful.

During the following years, I essentially raised myself with minimal guidance from my aunt and uncle. It was a unique dynamic, but they were my family. I grew close to them and their partners, who were also a meaningful part of my childhood. They provided me with much-needed guidance and stability; I loved and appreciated them.

As I approached the age of twelve, my aunt and uncle married and started their lives with their respective spouses. In the wake of this new chapter, I found myself left behind in the abandoned Hancock Court house, a symbol of my fractured existence. There, I encountered my deepest fears and insecurities, wrestling with the belief that everyone I loved would eventually leave me.

When my parents eventually moved into the Hancock house, it felt like I was there by default rather than by choice. The household lacked the warmth and comfort I had known with Mama, making the transition even more challenging. I immersed myself in schoolwork, excelling there and eventually becoming an overachiever to distract myself from the loneliness at home.

For me, it felt as though I was merely an afterthought, a mere observer in the lives of those who were supposed to provide love and stability. I have my biological father's last name, which already brought me shame, but it was nothing compared to not having the same name as anyone in my house or anyone I knew, for that matter. I didn't even know how to pronounce my last name correctly until I met my siblings. I was three shades darker than everyone else in my household, and my brother and I have a nine-year age difference. I felt and looked like the family nanny, and often, I bonded more with her than with my parents.

These childhood experiences greatly influenced my perception of self-worth and relationships. The wounds of abandonment and rejection left me with a deep-rooted belief that I was undeserving of love and acceptance. This belief subconsciously drove me to seek validation, often through accomplishments, unhealthy patterns, and poor choices.

Seeking love and approval became a complicated maze, leading me down dark paths that only deepened my pain. The void left by my absent father fueled a desperate need for male attention, often resulting in toxic relationships that were emotionally, mentally, or physically abusive. My constant search for external validation drove impulsive decisions as I tried to fill the emptiness inside.

It took years to realize I had been seeking love in all the wrong places, hoping others could give me what I could only find within myself. For so long, I believed I wasn't enough—perhaps God had abandoned me too. But over time, His presence became clear, reshaping how I saw myself and my worth.

For so long, I believed love was something I had to chase or earn, something that would always slip away. But in the quiet moments, when I finally listened, I found a love that didn't leave. God was there, steady and unwavering, showing me that I was always enough. Slowly, I began to heal.

"The Lord will lead you. He himself is with you. He will not fail you or leave you. Don't worry. Don't be afraid!"

Deuteronomy 31:8 ERV

AWAKEN & Reflect

My past does not define me, but it can offer valuable
wisdom. I will reflect with kindness toward myself
and an open heart for growth.

AWARENESS:

How have my past experiences shaped
the way I see myself and my worth?

_____

_____

_____

_____

_____

_____

_____

_____

_____

_____

_____

_____

_____

_____

_____

_____

_____

_____

_____

WORK IT:

What is one step I can take to shift from seeking external validation to recognizing my own worth?

_____

_____

_____

_____

_____

_____

_____

_____

_____

_____

_____

_____

_____

_____

_____

_____

_____

_____

_____

_____

_____

ALIGNMENT:

When have I felt lost or uncertain?
What helped me move forward?

_____

_____

_____

_____

_____

_____

_____

_____

_____

_____

_____

_____

_____

_____

_____

_____

_____

_____

KNOWLEDGE:

What insights have my difficult seasons given
me about resilience and self-love?

_____

_____

_____

_____

_____

_____

_____

_____

_____

_____

_____

_____

_____

_____

_____

_____

_____

_____

_____

_____

EMBRACE:

How can I begin accepting myself as I am,
without conditions or comparisons?

_____

_____

_____

_____

_____

_____

_____

_____

_____

_____

_____

_____

_____

_____

_____

_____

_____

_____

_____

NAVIGATE:

What is one small way I can choose
self-compassion over self-criticism today?

_____

_____

_____

_____

_____

_____

_____

_____

_____

_____

_____

_____

_____

_____

_____

_____

"FORGET THE FORMER THINGS; DO NOT DWELL ON THE PAST.
SEE, I AM DOING A NEW THING!"
– ISAIAH 43:18-19

CHAPTER THREE

MISGUIDED PURSUITS

As I sit here reflecting on my tainted relationship with Mike, I can't help but feel a mix of emotions. He is my oldest friend. I honestly met Mike when I probably needed him most. I was still having panic attacks when I arrived at school after my mom or my grandma left me there. I had just mastered getting through my Kindergarten days, and suddenly, I had to stay in school longer. It was embarrassing how much I cried for reasons I couldn't explain. Mike was the class clown. Whatever he did or said that day, I can't recall, but I knew I was thankful that he distracted me from my fears and insecurities.

We were reunited in middle school, and by then, Mike had already gained a reputation as a bit of a player, even at such a young age, but he was persistent in pursuing me, eventually leading to us becoming a couple in our first year of high school. I was fourteen.

Mike was my first everything. My first real boyfriend, my first serious relationship, and, unfortunately, my first experience with trauma bonding, unhealthy attachments, and toxic coping skills. Looking back, I now realize that our connection was based on seeking love and attention from each other, filling the void left by absent parents. We both longed for the love and validation we never received at home and found solace in each other's arms and beds.

But our relationship was far from healthy. We were like the rapper Eminem and his ex-wife Kim, or Yvette and Jodi (from *Baby Boy*)—constantly oscillating between love and hate, passion and aggression. We matched each other's energy in happiness as well as in toxic ways, and it weighed heavily on both of us emotionally. It wasn't just about the love and attention we sought, though.

Our relationship also involved experimenting with risky behaviors like smoking weed and sneaking out. I can't speak for him on his reason for doing these things, but I identify this time in my life as a mechanism for coping with my frustration and sadness and the beginning of my addictive personality. We were rebellious teenagers trying to escape our pain, and we found comfort in each other.

Then there was the infidelity. I was consumed by rage that I could not control. The first time I learned that Mike had cheated on me, my immediate response was: "The audacity of this mother fucker!" I went with a friend to find Mike at his friend's house, getting ready to work out. In the midst of him getting ready to lift the bench press bar, I climbed on top of him in a seductive, straddling position, distracted him as though I wanted to get cute and sexual, and then hit him directly in his chest.

I felt betrayed and blamed myself for not contacting him when I woke up that day as I usually would have. I believed that if I didn't attempt to play games about who likes who more, who calls who first type of shit, then he wouldn't have had the time or desire to hook up with one of my friends. It took a long time before I realized it was not my fault that he wandered. I didn't know better. *Is this love?*

It was a constant cycle of breaking up and getting back together, and strangely enough, I found comfort in the predictability of it all. We were together, everyone knew it, we were Mike and Aisa. Yet, he went to a Homecoming Dance with someone else. After the dance, we all drove to the nearby Denny's. His date Monica, of course, wanted to be bold and talk all kinds of shit to me. As I was in the driver's seat of my red Honda Accord (Mike and I had matching cars, too, eye roll), sticking my head out of the window screaming at him, Monica suddenly came up and smacked me in the face. I don't even remember reacting to her; I just recall yelling at Mike to "Get in my fucking car!"

Micah and Kristina were in my backseat, watching everything go down unexpectedly. Mike got in the passenger seat, and I drove to the gas station across the street. I parked my car and just started swinging.

Shortly after, a police officer parked behind my car. My heart was racing. Palms were sweating. I had never been in any kind of trouble before.

"Please step out of your vehicle," the officer said. "I had received a call about a rumble happening in the gas station parking lot."

He shone his flashlight directly towards my face. It was intimidating. He asked me if Mike did that. My cheek was already swelling from Monica's sudden slap in the face, and ironically, for reasons I don't remember, my mom had smacked me on the same cheek hours before the dance.

The officer advised me that I was free to go. Thank

God. I think I left Mike behind. I took the girls home and shortly after ended up meeting Anthony at another of our friends' houses and getting high with them. My unhealthy coping skills and disassociation attempts likely started, or were magnified, during this period.

There were times when I had pregnancy scares during my junior or senior year, and Mike was too much of an asshole to care enough to take me to the clinic. I wasn't driving at the time. By then, Anthony had proven to be a reliable friend. He was one of the first in our group of friends to drive. Whether he was ditching or didn't have a class, he was always willing to take me where I needed to go. I appreciated him, especially when Mike should've been there. I eventually referred to Anthony as my Best Friend. In case I didn't mention it, Best Friend also became Charlotte's dad, but we'll get into that again later.

Despite Mike's infidelity, lies, and toxic measures, I believed that deep down, he loved me, and I convinced myself that I could fix whatever problems we had. I was wrong. Mike took pleasure in what seemed like the attention of how intense we were with one another. He liked it when people thought I was crazy and enjoyed the fact that I would fight them, or him, if necessary. I admit I eventually became accustomed to it, too. We didn't know better.

There was a time when he went through my agenda to find comments about how I went to see Anthony to pick up his old loveseat for my new apartment near campus. Mike woke me up in the middle of the night, upset beyond measure, demanding I get into his car. No time to put pants on or grab a jacket, just a tank top and panties. As he questioned me in his car, driving recklessly with anger, he rolled down the windows and the moonroof. He wanted me to freeze until I admitted what he found in my journal and to punish me as he drove to what looked like the middle of nowhere.

Sometimes, he abandoned me in another city, and I was left to find a ride home just because he was mad. Uber did not exist yet. Mike is the friend I've known the longest, and with his awareness of the most profound childhood wounds from my dad being a cheater and abandoning my mom and me, I could not fathom why he was so quick to treat me this way.

Why didn't he believe I was worthy of respect and fidelity? Or, more importantly, why did I not deserve the truth from him? Please tell me your real issues and let me decide if I want to stay or go. Regardless, I wasn't wise enough, or strong enough, to officially cut him off.

Instead, I matched his energy and justified my behavior and our relationship by seeking attention from other guys. There were times when I genuinely wanted to move on and be open to the good things I saw in others I talked to along the way, but no one was willing to take me seriously at the end of the day because I always ended up back with Mike. It felt so hard to break free.

Everything changed during my first semester at California State University, Fullerton. I was taking on a heavy course load, 23 units to be exact, and the stress was eating away at me. On the day of my Economics 101 final, I distinctly remember the nearby Carl's Jr. stench that nauseated me. I couldn't concentrate in class. Something felt off. I had a gut instinct. I ran to take a pregnancy test at the campus health center immediately after class. It came back positive.

I was terrified. I confided in my cousin, who then directed me to her older sister for guidance. They assured me that they would support me no matter my decision. The reality was that I was only seventeen years old, and my life was just beginning. I had dreams and ambitions that I couldn't let go of. Deep down, I knew I wasn't ready to become a mother, especially with Mike by my side, who pretended to want to be a dad but constantly sought attention elsewhere. And I was certain that my parents would disown me.

I debated and deliberated, taking time to reflect at my cousin's place by the beach, waiting from when I found out in November to the very last day in January to decide. But finally, seeing a hickey on Mike's neck during foreplay as he tried to paint this beautiful picture of how he would take care of me simply made me realize he would never be good to me, baby or not. That was the final straw.

In the end, I made an appointment with Planned Parenthood. It was a choice that haunted me for twenty years, but looking back, I know it was the right decision for me at that time. I didn't have the resources or support to provide for a child while trying to figure out my path. The aftermath of the abortion marked a turning point for me. I vowed to myself that I was done with him and felt some peace for the first time in a long while.

My decision had a profound impact on my life, an impact that I didn't fully comprehend until later in my adulthood. As painful as those experiences were, despite the amount of guilt and shame I carried for so many years, they shaped me and taught me valuable lessons about love, self-worth, and the importance of making choices that align with my whole well-being.

And so, I closed the chapter on Mike and Aisa and our toxic relationship. It was a difficult and dysfunctional journey, but one that ultimately led me to a path of healing and self-discovery. I swore to seek love in healthier places, prioritize my happiness, and never settle for anything less than I deserved.

I AM LOVED—
"YES, I AM SURE THAT NOTHING
CAN SEPARATE US FROM GOD'S
LOVE—NOT DEATH, LIFE,
ANGELS, OR RULING SPIRITS."

ROMANS 8:38 ERV

AWAKEN & *Reflect*

Every experience—good or painful—has something to teach me. I will approach these reflections with an open heart and the belief that healing is possible.

AWARENESS:

How have past decisions, made from
pain or fear, shaped my growth?

_____

_____

_____

_____

_____

_____

_____

_____

_____

_____

_____

_____

_____

_____

_____

_____

_____

_____

_____

_____

_____

WORK IT:

How can I release guilt or shame and embrace grace as part of my healing process?

_____

_____

_____

_____

_____

_____

_____

_____

_____

_____

_____

_____

_____

_____

_____

_____

_____

_____

_____

_____

ALIGNMENT:

What does self-honoring love look like for me, and how can I practice it?

_____

_____

_____

_____

_____

_____

_____

_____

_____

_____

_____

_____

_____

_____

_____

_____

_____

_____

_____

_____

_____

_____

KNOWLEDGE:

What lessons have past mistakes taught me about self-worth and making aligned choices?

_____

_____

_____

_____

_____

_____

_____

_____

_____

_____

_____

_____

_____

_____

_____

_____

_____

_____

_____

EMBRACE:

How can I remind myself that I am deeply loved,
no matter my past?

_____

_____

_____

_____

_____

_____

_____

_____

_____

_____

_____

_____

_____

_____

_____

_____

_____

_____

_____

NAVIGATE:

What is one intentional step I can take today
to prioritize my happiness and never
settle for less than I deserve?

_____

_____

_____

_____

_____

_____

_____

_____

_____

_____

_____

_____

_____

_____

_____

"WE KNOW THAT IN ALL THINGS GOD WORKS FOR THE GOOD
OF THOSE WHO LOVE HIM, WHO HAVE BEEN
CALLED ACCORDING TO HIS PURPOSE."
— ROMANS 8:28

CHAPTER FOUR

SUBTLE TEMPTATIONS

I vividly remember my first time hitting the pipe. We were in Anthony's garage, sitting in the backseat of my old, silver Toyota Matrix. At that moment, I was supposed to be heading to class in Fullerton, but the fascination of trying something new overcame me. Anthony asked if I wanted a little motivation before I went, and without much hesitation, I agreed.

"Hmmm... in that case," my overachieving, dumb-ass self said, "why not?" I didn't need much convincing. I listened carefully and followed his instructions.

"Now," he said, signaling me to inhale as he gently twisted the glass pipe side to side with his fingertips.

I sucked slowly, inhaled, and gradually started enjoying this elated sensation that began to take hold of me. There was no coughing or choking. It was very different from smoking weed. The effects crept up subtly, just like the enemy. My mouth had a slight aftertaste and a weird feeling, but that was it. I should have known; I was fucked from that moment. It does that to you.

That day, completely unaware of the havoc it would wreak on my life, I experienced a surge in productivity. I aced a psychology midterm, did laundry, and felt like I had accomplished so much with little effort. But along with these initial highs came the first signs of the lows, but I knew nothing of withdrawals yet. I stayed awake for three days straight, my mind racing and my body restless. My appetite disappeared, and the thought of eating anything except liquids was nauseating; duly noted. It should have been a wake-up call, a glimpse into the grip this substance would have on me. But the bad didn't outweigh the good, so fuck it.

Fast forward two and a half years, and my addiction spiraled out of control. I found myself entangled in a web of lies, telling my parents I lived near campus when, in reality, I resided just a few miles away with Anthony, and I was bold enough to live in the same community as some of my family members. I eventually isolated myself from friends and family; I chose to give in to the temptation of the drug and spend my days in bed with him instead.

My academic performance wasn't significantly impacted, which I considered a personal key indicator of my success. I kept up appearances by occasionally attending classes and meticulously cleaning our apartment to create the façade of a stable home. Still, it was only a matter of time before our addiction inevitably took over us.

Financial troubles soon followed. They say never to get high on your own supply, right? Well, he sold it, and we consumed it. Desperate for money to support our habit, I resorted to stealing high-end clothes and returned them for cash. I even went as far as selling my own blood plasma multiple times. The cycle of addiction had taken over my life, and I felt like I was losing all sense of control.

Amidst the chaos, I realized that this wasn't the life I wanted. I reached out for help and sought counseling at the health center on campus again. Thank you, Lord, for my desire to seek out my resources. Although unsure if my problem was severe enough for rehab, I knew I couldn't continue down this destructive path. The therapist provided resources, and I set out to make a change with newfound determination.

I approached Anthony with a proposition—we needed to get clean together. However, he suggested that we consume what was left before quitting. I was in absolute agreement; it does that to you. Little did I know that this decision would lead us to spin directly to our rock bottom. The aftermath of our withdrawals was devastating. My appetite vanished, my eyes dilated, and my vision became blurred. Paranoia crept in, fueling fights and distrust. Clearly, we were losing control of our lives and minds.

Anthony's possessiveness and aggressive behavior escalated during this time. He would lock me out of our bedroom so he could come down alone, blocking the door with filing cabinets and parts of our wooden bedframe. He went through my phone and interrogated me. He once threw my phone out of my car, displaying a toxic level of jealousy. He behaved with an air of grandiose invincibility. Our relationship deteriorated, and things took a violent turn. He left bruises on my arms, and I realized it was time to seek help.

I made the difficult decision to call the police, but to be completely transparent, it was more of an impulsive decision, knowing that we were both completely out of control, not because I was scared he would hurt me. Anthony was arrested, and I made immediate moves toward recovery. June 2005 marks my Turning a New Leaf period—no more drugs, stealing, or lies, nothing.

I made the mistake of confiding in my cousins again. This time, I didn't need help making a decision; instead, I hoped my cousin's boyfriend would help me move the furniture out of our apartment. I figured I could move back home like my mom wanted since it was summer break. I decided to sell all my furniture to pay off the credit card I had used to buy it. Little did I know, my cousin took it upon herself to rat me out, and I was summoned to my aunt's house. I knew something was going on. A part of me considered driving far away and never coming back. I knew they were plotting against me. I walked into the house, and sure enough, there was a whole family intervention.

Determined to turn my life around, I sought help and ended up at a county rehab center. I think that's what my mom's insurance covered, or perhaps she just went with the first one she found. Regardless, I was sure that I was in the wrong place. The environment didn't feel right. It seemed filled with people who were there due to court orders or for forced treatment. I knew I needed a different approach.

My roommate at the facility seemed a lot older and wiser than my 19-year-old self. She suggested I seek treatment at the Loma Linda University Behavioral Medical Center. This outpatient program specializes in dual diagnosis, addressing both chemical dependency and mental health issues such as depression or bipolar disorder. Realizing that this could be the fresh start I needed and the approach I may be yearning for, I decided to leave the county rehab and register for the three-month program at Loma Linda.

My time at the Loma Linda University BMC was transformational. The program integrated various therapeutic modalities, with Cognitive Behavioral Therapy (CBT) being particularly impactful. Additionally, the program included practicing breathing techniques, arts and crafts, and sessions with the chaplain. Initially, I viewed the arts and crafts as trivial, but I've since embraced it over the years as a valuable part of my self-care routine, helping me stay grounded and relaxed as I express my creativity.

Cognitive behavioral therapy resonated with me greatly, providing me with the tools I needed to overcome addiction. I learned to understand that my addiction stemmed from years of deeper issues I had been avoiding or trying to escape.

Surrendering to the process and embracing the 12 steps became pivotal in my recovery. It all started with a few love-and-hate letters, and the healing began to take effect. Their first assignment was to ask three people I trusted to write a letter or list of 20 affirmations of me. Often, recovering people with an addiction, as well as regular individuals, may find it challenging to recognize and celebrate their own attributes, so asking someone else to do it for you is a phenomenal way to borrow their belief until you have it for yourself.

06/20/2005

I took care of Aisa since birth, she's always been a caring, lovable and sweet child. I have so much trust and faith in her because I know she is very smart, intelligent, ambitious and most of all a fighter. In addition, Aisa is a very reliable person. When Aisa was living with me, I could always count on her. She follows and obeys my rules. For example, her chores are always done in a timely manner. She cleans the house, feeds and bathes the dog. Aisa is also a responsible sister. She takes care of her brother whenever she's out of school. She feeds him, helps with his homework and plays with him. Aisa tries to work hard to stand on her own, to meet her needs and also tries her best to handle her own personal issues because she is able to make decisions under stress. Aisa is very outspoken and open-minded, ever since before, we can always sit together and talk about her problems.

Aisa grew up under my care. If there's anybody that really knows Aisa that would be me. I always have faith in her in spite of any obstacles that she has to go through, to prove to herself and everybody that she can turn everything around for a better future.

-Lola Mama (grandma)

It really did amaze me how well Mama and I communicated. Being the oldest Filipino I knew, it was ironic that I learned how to understand Tagalog and a few other dialects Mama spoke, yet Mama talked to me in English for as long as I can remember. I didn't have to talk louder as she got older. I didn't have to speak more appropriately than my authentic self. I didn't have to slow down when I shared stories, and I never had to sugarcoat anything because she always gave the same in return. I miss her.

One of my most detailed memories of her was sitting at her round, glass kitchen table. She didn't scold me about the drugs. She asked me questions. She understood my pain. She shared with me family insight, details that prove our family's generational curses and lies that have come and gone. I don't quite know or understand why she shared the stories with me, but I learned from her that we all have a story. Some people have skeletons in their closets. Meanwhile, others share their stories to be a light. Thank you, Mama.

In August 2005, I successfully completed the program at Loma Linda Behavioral Medical Center. Although challenging, I emerged stronger and more determined than ever before.

I am Saved—
"The temptations in your life are no different from what others experience. And God is faithful. He will not allow the temptation to be more than you can stand."

1 Corinthians 10:13 NLT

AWAKEN & *Reflect*

I will approach my challenges, habits, and
distractions with self-compassion and a
willingness to grow, rather than judgment.

AWARENESS:

What habits, distractions, or coping
mechanisms have I used to numb pain
or escape difficult emotions?

_____

_____

_____

_____

_____

_____

_____

_____

_____

_____

_____

_____

_____

_____

_____

_____

_____

_____

WORK IT:

When facing temptation or unhealthy patterns,
what has helped me regain control
or choose a different path?

_____

_____

_____

_____

_____

_____

_____

_____

_____

_____

_____

_____

_____

_____

_____

_____

_____

ALIGNMENT:

Who in my life has supported or
believed in me during my struggles?
How can I lean into that encouragement?

_____

_____

_____

_____

_____

_____

_____

_____

_____

_____

_____

_____

_____

_____

_____

_____

_____

_____

KNOWLEDGE:

What lessons have my past challenges taught me
about resilience, self-worth, or healing?

_____
_____
_____
_____
_____
_____
_____
_____
_____
_____
_____
_____
_____
_____
_____
_____
_____
_____
_____

EMBRACE:

How can I extend grace and compassion to
myself as I navigate personal growth?

_____

_____

_____

_____

_____

_____

_____

_____

_____

_____

_____

_____

_____

_____

_____

_____

NAVIGATE:

What is one daily practice I can commit to that
nourishes my mind, body, or spirit?

_____

_____

_____

_____

_____

_____

_____

_____

_____

_____

_____

_____

_____

_____

_____

_____

"WATCH AND PRAY SO THAT YOU WILL NOT FALL INTO
TEMPTATION. THE SPIRIT IS WILLING, BUT THE FLESH IS WEAK."
– MATTHEW 26:41

CHAPTER FIVE

FROM STRUGGLE TO SUCCESS

Reflecting on my journey from addiction to recovery, there were many obstacles and challenges I had to overcome. However, amidst the struggle, moments of divine intervention led me toward success and a newfound purpose in life.

During my time in the outpatient rehab program in June 2005, I began searching for job opportunities that would allow me to earn a living while continuing my recovery journey and focusing on school. I concentrated on finding a position as a receptionist in a hotel or a kiosk at the mall where I could work on my homework during slow shifts. While this seemed like a suitable option, little did I know that fate had a different plan in mind.

On my way to pay my bill at a Verizon Wireless store, I noticed the managers engaged in friendly conversation and displaying exceptional customer service skills. I took the initiative to ask if there were any job openings, and to my surprise, they confirmed that they were hiring and requested my resume. Thank you, God; I happened to have a resume with me in my car at that moment. It felt like God's hand at work, aligning the stars for an unexpected opportunity.

Subsequently, I went through the interview process while simultaneously attending my outpatient program. Work became necessary as I was essentially cut off and transitioned into a phase of financial independence, taking over responsibilities that my parents had once supported. With bills to pay and a desire to rebuild my life, I started my first entry-level career as an Assistant to Sales Operations at Verizon Wireless.

The adjustment from addiction to the corporate world was daunting initially. Still, I discovered that the skills I learned during my recovery journey and in college were applicable to this new environment. The discipline, resilience, and determination cultivated through overcoming addiction and my first two years at CSUF served as valuable assets. As for the outstanding customer service and sales skills required for success, that came naturally to me.

However, it's essential to acknowledge that the struggle with addiction wasn't entirely behind me. I relied on substitutions and sought satisfaction through different means. This manifested in various forms, such as an addiction to laxatives, diet pills, self-induced vomiting, and pain pills. These actions provided temporary relief, an escape from the pain and discomfort I was experiencing.

Looking back, I realize these behaviors stemmed from seeking solace and control through physical sensations. It wasn't about body dysmorphia or a quest for perfection but rather an attempt to numb or distract myself from internal struggles. These coping mechanisms took different forms throughout my journey, including ten tattoos, twelve piercings, and engaging in promiscuous behavior.

I eventually moved on from Verizon to work as a Personal Banker for Wells Fargo. As a full-time working mom, I faced numerous challenges and struggles. As the sole provider for my daughter Charlotte, I worked tirelessly to make ends meet, leaving little time for rest or personal fulfillment. Charlotte went to her dad's place one day per week, which became less frequent as she got older. The financial burden wore heavy on me, especially when it seemed that Anthony was not contributing as much as he should have.

During this time, I decided to surrender to my higher power and trust in God's provision. I finally grasped the idea that relying on my own efforts alone or depending on Anthony was not the plan. It took me even longer to realize that I needed to yield to God's will in its entirety. Relying on myself was not enough. I needed to place my faith in something greater than me. Understanding and believing that God would care for Charlotte and me became my source of strength and comfort.

Throughout this period, my living situation was constantly changing. We moved from living with my mom after the separation to getting our own apartment in Rancho Cucamonga, to living in a tri-level condo in Ontario, and having roommates for the first time. We've downsized and upgraded several times throughout the years. Unfortunately, some of these roommate experiences turned out to be horror stories, adding to the difficulties I faced as a mom trying to juggle everything. Other times, however, God strategically put the perfect roommates and gracious landlords in place at just the right time in our lives.

The daily challenges of being a single, full-time working mom deeply affected my mental and emotional state. I often felt overwhelmed by the never-ending to-do list, scattered belongings, and the pressure to attend after-school activities while ensuring my daughter was happy, healthy, and fed. Not to mention the tantrums, attitude, and meltdowns I had to endure. It was during this period that I discovered the value of support groups and classes designed specifically for single moms like me.

I enrolled Charlotte in a Divorce CARE for Kids class, which helped us both navigate the challenging conversations about parents not living together as Charlotte began to ask questions and compare our home and family dynamic to those of her friends. It was a relief to have access to guidance and answers that I had struggled to provide her on my own. I also became involved in a Single Moms Ministry and participated in various activities at church. These connections provided both the practical support and the spiritual guidance that I desperately needed during that time.

While pouring everything into work and caring for Charlotte, love and relationships took a backseat. I consciously avoided adding any additional stress to my life and focused solely on providing for my daughter and building a stable future for us. It was a time of self-preservation, where I prioritized our well-being above all else.

However, in 2013, a tragic event shifted my perspective once again. Mike, Charlotte's grandfather, an impactful person in our lives and the person with whom we lived briefly after Anthony and I separated, unexpectedly passed away. We received the devastating news while attending Charlotte's Christmas performance, and despite rushing to the hospital, we arrived too late to say our final goodbyes.

This loss hit Anthony hard, as Mike was his stepdad. Witnessing Anthony's pain and realizing that I couldn't offer any support or reassurance to him was challenging, but he wasn't the only one who was heartbroken and grieving.

Why was I so affected? I felt lost. Whether it was due to his loving support when we lived with him, the turning point in my career, the impending approach of my 30s, or the lack of fulfillment in my workplace, I was battling with a sense of emptiness.

Grieving Mike's passing was a crucial part of my healing journey. Although he wasn't an immediate family member, he was very much a father figure to me. I needed time to reflect, heal, and find my way forward. Unfortunately, I wasn't permitted to take bereavement leave from Wells Fargo since Mike wasn't my biological father, which only intensified the already overwhelming emotions I was experiencing. My branch manager at the time, who was also a longtime mentor and close friend, responded with his usual compassion and understanding. We agreed that once I met my compensation sales quota for the quarter, he would approve the use of my available PTO/vacation hours, allowing me to take the time I needed. I achieved my goals, and I was gone for a month to grieve. Thank you, God, and Bobby, too.

There was one day I struggled with in particular. I can't recall what led to the sudden urges. It could have been the result of binge-watching *Breaking Bad* on Netflix for the first time, but I definitely needed a Narcotics Anonymous meeting. It had been eight years since I last went to a meeting.

I saw a couple verbally and physically fighting outside the building. I saw people coming in for the first time, still spun out of their minds. I saw others putting their court orders on the table to be signed. I wasn't trying to judge them. I was them, at one point. It was a rude awakening and such a humbling experience; it reminded me that addiction and relapse were no longer a part of my identity.

I moved through this period of grief with a lot of questioning. Something about Mike's sudden death propelled me to discover my purpose and not waste time on what I thought were my desires for my life and career. I began going to the gym every morning to get my mind right. I developed a passion for hiking as I would listen to worship music, cry as I felt necessary, and go to my mountain top and pray to God every morning to bless me with the clarity I needed and the career that would allow me to live with passion and purpose. I didn't know what that meant yet, nor what it looked like. I was only certain I was meant to impact lives on a grander scale and deeper level; I knew my destiny was more than teaching financial literacy, offering budgeting techniques, and cross-selling all of Wells Fargo Bank's financial products.

I continued to attend church, seeking solace in small groups and serving in the children's ministry. Although I was still new to Christianity and figuring out how to practice my faith, I felt confident that I didn't need to memorize scripture to love and pray for the one- and two-year-olds in my care. I kept an open mind, recognizing the importance of guidance and support in my spiritual journey.

As I learned in my recovery from addiction, consistency and perseverance are vital in finding healing and purpose. So I kept returning to the places that brought me peace and comfort while leveraging the many tools in my toolbox. *It truly works, if you work it.* I spent a lot of time self-reflecting and crying on those mountaintops, having conversations with God, taking inventory of my gifts and passions, contemplating my transferable skills. By April 2014, I made the brave decision to leave financial services and transition to becoming an Engineering & Environmental Recruiter with Aerotek Recruiting and Staffing.

To all those who feel lost, stuck, or hopeless in the depths of self-discovery, I challenge you to embrace the power of surrender and faith. When faced with the daunting task of understanding our purpose, it is crucial to turn to our Creator and seek His guidance and a deeper connection with Him. Ask God to reveal His plan for your life, to illuminate the path that leads to fulfilling His desires and serving others with love and compassion. Trust in His infinite wisdom and believe that He will guide you every step of the way. Remember, true fulfillment lies not in pursuing selfish ambitions but in aligning our lives with the divine purpose for which we were created.

"For I know the plans I have for you," says the Lord. "They are plans for good and not for disaster, to give you a future and a hope."

Jeremiah 29:11 NLT

AWAKEN & *Reflect*

Growth is a journey, not a destination.
I will reflect on my next steps while
honoring how far I've already come.

AWARENESS:

In what areas of my life do I feel lost, stuck, or
uncertain about what comes next?

_____

_____

_____

_____

_____

_____

_____

_____

_____

_____

_____

_____

_____

_____

_____

_____

_____

_____

_____

_____

WORK IT:

How have my past struggles shaped the way I approach new opportunities and challenges?

_____

_____

_____

_____

_____

_____

_____

_____

_____

_____

_____

_____

_____

_____

_____

_____

_____

_____

_____

_____

ALIGNMENT:

What does living a life of peace, success, and
fulfillment look like for me right now?

_____

_____

_____

_____

_____

_____

_____

_____

_____

_____

_____

_____

_____

_____

_____

_____

_____

_____

_____

KNOWLEDGE:

What lessons have past transitions—whether
personal, professional, or spiritual—taught me
about resilience and trust?

_____

_____

_____

_____

_____

_____

_____

_____

_____

_____

_____

_____

_____

_____

_____

_____

_____

_____

_____

EMBRACE:

How can I trust that I am exactly where
I need to be in this moment, even if
I don't see the full picture yet?

_____

_____

_____

_____

_____

_____

_____

_____

_____

_____

_____

_____

_____

_____

_____

_____

_____

_____

_____

_____

NAVIGATE:

What is one small step I can take today
to move forward with faith and confidence
in the journey ahead?

_____

_____

_____

_____

_____

_____

_____

_____

_____

_____

_____

_____

_____

_____

_____

_____

"COMMIT TO THE LORD WHATEVER YOU DO, AND HE WILL
ESTABLISH YOUR PLANS."
— PROVERBS 16:3

CHAPTER SIX

THAT ENTREPRENEUR LIFE

As a child, falling asleep in any moving vehicle became second nature, a habit I couldn't shake. But it wasn't until my early college days that exhaustion started hitting hard. Between taking 23 units my first semester, part-time jobs between the Titan Student Union and Macy's, and the occasional late-night partying, I relied heavily on carpooling, coffee, and 5-Hour Energy shots to keep me going, assuming that the uncontrollable sleep spells in class or while stuck in traffic were entirely normal for a college student my age. Thinking back on those years, it became evident that perhaps my addiction to methamphetamines was caused by my attempt to self-medicate the sleeping disorder I didn't know I had.

In 2017, in my early thirties, the brain fog in my mind thickened, and staying awake became a daily struggle. It wasn't just a nuisance anymore but a danger to myself and others, as I would often doze off at the wheel if I drove for more than thirty minutes. That's when I finally sought help, went through my first sleep study, and was diagnosed with hypersomnolence. I was prescribed Adderall, offering temporary relief, but its effects didn't last.

12/31/17

New Year's Eve Letter

God, our heavenly father, first and foremost, Thank you! Thank you for being so faithful. I have had many challenges and sometimes make the wrong choices, but you have always been faithful. Thank you, Lord.

Thank you for my new home. Please bless our home, protect it and everything in it. Please keep Charlotte and me safe from the enemy and temptation and, most importantly, from our world's distractions.

Please bless my job, my work, and my success. Again, I have seen how faithful you are, and as we now have this expensive home and responsibility, I worry if my job does not work out. Or I am not diligent with my spending. So, God, please help me.

Please guide, direct, and help me do things right and in the way you want me to. Please help me raise Charlotte the way you want me to. Please help me teach her the way you intended. I need your help, Lord.

I struggle with my own issues as I try to do my best to raise her, which is so hard! Especially alone. I pray that she learns obedience, respect, and kindness.

Thank you, Lord, for my family and friends. And especially for bringing my mom and me to a better place again. I pray Mama will be happy. Lastly, Lord, I pray that you bless me with a Godly man and that I make good choices about love and relationships. In Jesus' name, Amen!

I prayed for this moment many times, and finally, God began to bless me abundantly. I upgraded and got myself a Lexus without needing a co-signer, defying expectations based on my previous financial challenges after my separation from Anthony. I had finally achieved a sense of stability. My daughter and I moved into the ideal townhome that provided us with the much-needed space and comfort we needed, and God blessed us with an amazing landlord who was a gracious and understanding mother figure. Gone were the days of sharing a bedroom and a queen-sized bed; we now had two master suites, a backyard for our beloved fur kiddos, and a newfound sense of security. That townhome on Summerfield, with its stairs that Charlotte had longed for for years, felt like home. Something about it made us feel safer, and it became our sanctuary—a place to build a promise-filled life. It was a testament to how far we had come from our humble beginnings.

During this time, I decided to take a daring leap into entrepreneurship. Like most of my career moves, I was approached by a professional headhunter who offered me an incredible opportunity to work with a recruitment company as my own boss. We both came from the world of Robert Half Staffing, so I knew we spoke the same language. I saw the value in the opportunity to partner with a company that was more aligned with my personal and professional goals.

In February 2018, I left Corporate America as a Healthcare Recruiter, and by March 2018, my first LLC was born—a venture that would prove to test my resilience, creativity, and purpose. Little did I know that this decision would shape my professional life and my journey of identity, love, and health.

In July 2018, I reconnected with someone I had briefly met five years earlier. His older brother had introduced us, but at the time, he was 21 years old, and we didn't pursue a romantic relationship. As we caught up, he almost immediately mentioned how I had never allowed him to take me out on a date, as discussed years prior. Intrigued,

I entertained the possibility. This was the beginning of the "Mr. Jones" period—the good, bad, and ugly. But we'll get into that more later.

The summer of 2018 was a season of great optimism. My life seemed to fall into place; my prayers were slowly being answered, and I considered opening my heart to love again. However, life had other plans for me. Becoming self-employed also meant a change in my health insurance, meaning a change with my doctor as well.

"Thank you for explaining all of your symptoms in detail. We want to help you figure out the root cause of your hypersomnolence and not simply put a band-aid on your condition. However, since you mentioned falling asleep while you drive, despite taking your 15 mg of Adderall twice daily, and because we are state-mandated reporters, we will have to notify the DMV and revoke your driver's license," said the doctor I never met with again, whose name I don't even remember.

What in the actual fuck?!

Unexpectedly, during this initial, and only, visit with this particular doctor, he instantly revoked my driver's license, leaving me feeling bitter, angry, perplexed, and vulnerable. As a single mom, this devastating blow turned my whole world upside down, challenging my independence and entire being, forcing me to adapt, stretch, and grow into who I was called to be.

The following years brought radical transformations, shaping my life in ways I could never have anticipated. I encountered countless hurdles that tested my resilience, pushing me to the brink of my capabilities. It often felt like tending to a garden, where I had to nurture and cultivate my growth surrounded by challenges, with each obstacle representing a new seedling to tend and my roots expanding in the dark.

During this difficult period of soul-searching, I experienced a powerful revelation in my sense of self. Losing my driver's license became a pivotal moment in my journey of self-discovery. I surrendered my Lexus to the bank, which, on your credit, is nearly as damaging as a repossession. Charlotte and I began relying on Instacart, Uber Eats, and Doordash. I became an expert with our Metrolink train system, rideshares like Uber and Lyft and the best routes for walking. I carefully chose our errands to manage the high cost of these services and ability to carry our purchases to our next destination.

The most difficult transition was probably being forced to pull Charlotte out of her elementary school which was too far to walk and having no other form of transportation, resulting in homeschooling her during her formative years in middle school. It was similar to the experiences many had during COVID-19, but this was our reality two years earlier.

Daily work productivity became almost non-existent. Realizing that I might need to divert my business focus because my condition was gradually worsening, I started an e-commerce store for mid-century and modern furniture and design consulting services. Rediscovering who I genuinely am, despite my conditions, brought forth various emotions, simultaneously dismantling and rebuilding my confidence and self-esteem over and over again. Despite my grit and ability to pivot my business endeavors, I felt lost, lonely, and defeated.

I joined a 12-step program at Water of Life to learn how to grieve my old, healthy self. Despite all of us attending for various reasons: addiction to food, sex, drugs, and codependency, we all related to each other, and I was exactly where I needed to be at the time.

Being self-employed, having exhausted what was available to me in California disability benefits and the very last of my savings, I believed that I had no choice but to return to a corporate job. I desperately needed stability again.

Instead of continuing to recruit for staffing agencies like Aerotek or Accountemps, or for start-ups as I had previously, I chose to work as a Talent Acquisition Manager for a construction management firm in Orange County.

In 2019, while working in the HR Department, I faced difficulties protecting my personal health information and deciding whether to disclose my health condition to my employer.

My concerns became a reality when I was unjustly terminated just a week after requesting reasonable accommodations to attend my doctor's appointments, highlighting the discrimination that many encounter in the workplace. Although I worked remotely three days a week, my request was reasonable. That day, I took the Metrolink train to the California Department of Fair Employment and Housing office in Santa Ana to file my complaint. I sought a skilled attorney experienced in such cases. This led to a lawsuit for wrongful termination, retaliation, and discrimination, which was settled in 2020.

Throughout these hardships, I remained steadfast, uncovering my resilience and determination. I believe that God guided me through these challenges to compel me to pause, slow down, and rely on Him rather than being consumed by the motions and distractions of this world. My journey with idiopathic hypersomnia, I feel, happened for a reason—to help others navigate similar struggles, whether they involve unexpected health situations, rare sleep disorders, or chronic illness. I began raising awareness about the complexities of this condition, becoming an advocate and a source of inspiration for those facing invisible illnesses.

I became a Rare Disease Legislative Advocate with RARE on the Road, a rare disease leadership series hosted by Global Genes and the EveryLife Foundation for Rare Diseases, providing critical education and insight into the rare disease community. During this time, I wrote and presented to Vice President Kamala Harris' office about Community Home Health & Telehealth Policies.

In 2021, I was accepted to participate in two cohorts with The RARE Compassion Program, which provides an opportunity for medical students to learn about the unique needs and challenges faced by individuals and their families living with undiagnosed or rare diseases. It was extremely rewarding to share my experiences across all areas of my life affected by my rare condition with the medical students I was partnered with. Building on this advocacy, in May 2024, I successfully petitioned the City of Rancho Cucamonga, California to issue a proclamation recognizing June 1st as Idiopathic Hypersomnia Awareness Day, further advancing awareness and support for this condition.

It hasn't been an easy road, but looking back, I realize the struggles and hardships were necessary for my growth. *I suffered. I learned. I changed.* Through self-reflection and introspection, I began peeling back the layers, uncovering hidden strengths and passions beneath my life's circumstances. Each setback became an opportunity for learning and a stepping stone to prepare me for God's plan.

I am on a continuous path of self-discovery, embracing the uncertainty and challenges it brings. Although immense difficulties have marked the past seven years, they have led to even more significant breakthroughs that have shaped me into who I am today. I am learning to understand my identity through the lens of my deeper purpose, and this journey has been a true awakening.

These experiences have allowed me to grow as an entrepreneur and, more importantly, as a servant leader, woman, and mother. I have realized that success is not defined exclusively by external achievements but by the inner growth and fulfillment that comes from aligning with my true passions, gifts, and values. Success is about discovering my true identity, developing my skills, and dominating my gifts to live a purpose-filled life.

As I continue my entrepreneurial journey, I am excited to discover what lies ahead. With each day, I gain a deeper understanding of who I am and what I am truly capable of. The road may be challenging, but I am confident that the lessons learned during this transformative period will guide me toward a future filled with joy, abundance, and a deep sense of fulfillment.

Self-discovery and entrepreneurial life are intertwined in ways I could not have predicted. Through embracing the challenges, setbacks, and triumphs, I am gradually unraveling the layers of my identity and embracing the person I am meant to become. This chapter is just the beginning of a lifelong journey of growth, empowerment, and self-actualization.

If you find yourself yearning for a sense of identity and purpose, I urge you to embark on the transformative journey of self-discovery. Reflect upon and take inventory of your passions, gifts, and values; seek out experiences that challenge and inspire you. Embrace the unknown and step outside your comfort zone, for we often find our true selves in uncertainty. Surround yourself with supportive individuals who uplift and encourage you along the way. Remember, self-discovery is not a destination but an ongoing process. Be patient, and show yourself compassion and grace as you navigate this path. Embrace the beauty of this journey, and let it empower you to live a life that fully embodies your essence.

"GOD HAS GIVEN EACH OF YOU A
GIFT FROM HIS GREAT VARIETY
OF SPIRITUAL GIFTS. USE THEM
WELL TO SERVE ONE ANOTHER."

1 PETER 4:10 NLT

AWAKEN & *Reflect*

Self-discovery is a lifelong journey.
I will be patient with myself as I evolve
in my own time, exactly as I am meant to.

AWARENESS:

What experiences—positive or challenging—have shaped my sense of identity and purpose?

_____

_____

_____

_____

_____

_____

_____

_____

_____

_____

_____

_____

_____

_____

_____

_____

_____

_____

WORK IT:

How can I reframe past setbacks as lessons that have prepared me for this season of growth?

_____

_____

_____

_____

_____

_____

_____

_____

_____

_____

_____

_____

_____

_____

_____

_____

_____

_____

_____

_____

ALIGNMENT:

What passions, gifts, or values feel most authentic to me, and how can I lean into them more?

_____

_____

_____

_____

_____

_____

_____

_____

_____

_____

_____

_____

_____

_____

_____

_____

_____

_____

_____

_____

_____

KNOWLEDGE:

Reflecting on my journey so far, what lessons have I learned about myself that I didn't expect?

_____

_____

_____

_____

_____

_____

_____

_____

_____

_____

_____

_____

_____

_____

_____

_____

_____

_____

_____

EMBRACE:

How can I practice patience and self-compassion as I
continue to evolve and step into my true self?

_____

_____

_____

_____

_____

_____

_____

_____

_____

_____

_____

_____

_____

_____

_____

_____

_____

_____

_____

_____

NAVIGATE:

What is one action I can take today to move forward in alignment with the person I am becoming?

_____

_____

_____

_____

_____

_____

_____

_____

_____

_____

_____

_____

_____

_____

_____

_____

_____

"TAKE DELIGHT IN THE LORD, AND HE WILL
GIVE YOU THE DESIRES OF YOUR HEART."
– PSALM 37:4

CHAPTER SEVEN

HOODWINKED

During my time as a personal banker, I formed a close bond with one of the tellers, a former co-worker who quickly became a trusted confidant. As single parents with daughters around the same age, we connected over the shared struggles of co-parenting, navigating the complexities of raising children while managing our own emotions. He was also a Christian who seemed to have grown up in the church and often shared godly wisdom that resonated with the season of life I was in—trying to master single motherhood while wrestling with my frustration toward my daughter's father.

He had tried to introduce me to his younger brother, Mr. Jones, on multiple occasions, but I wasn't interested when we first met. I was in the midst of a 13-month celibacy journey—intentionally dedicating that season to rediscovering my worth, deepening my relationship with God, and understanding who I was beyond any romantic or lustful connection. Five years later, I slid into Mr.

Jones' DMs—but not for the reason you might think. At the time, I was recruiting for a research and development chef position at King's Hawaiian and was headhunting for candidate referrals; so I messaged him on Instagram. He replied promptly and wasted no time reminding me about the date I never let him take me on. I'll admit, I was halfway flattered.

It made me pause and wonder, *God, am I supposed to be open-minded this time? Is there a reason we reconnected after all these years if You didn't have a plan for us?*

We met for drinks at a sports bar called Cruisers in Huntington Beach. I was house-sitting for my best friend, and I took it as a sign that our timing was right—confirmation, even. I was notorious for not making immediate plans with people, always busy and running around. But meeting with him felt different. It was the first time in eight years that I was willing to be open-minded about a relationship again, and somehow, our plans fell into place almost effortlessly.

The strong connection, the friendship, and the familiarity of knowing about his life through his brother and our conversations all led me to believe that maybe—just maybe—Mr. Jones was the man God had sent me, the one I had been praying for.

Why did we seem so happy? Why did we connect so effortlessly? Why did he have to hit it off so well with my daughter? She really liked him, and that made my heart happy. I didn't know any better.

I unintentionally introduced him to Charlotte on our second or third date. He came with me to pick her up from Vacation Bible School. Before Mr. Jones, Charlotte had met plenty of men I was friends with or worked with, but she had never met anyone I dated. The fact that she warmed to him so quickly reassured me. I had no concerns then.

He was a fun uncle to his niece, just like my brother was to Charlotte, so I assumed he was just naturally good with kids. He was a chef at a DoubleTree hotel—a huge win for me since I don't cook—and he quickly scored points with Charlotte by bringing her canisters of their famous chocolate chip cookies.

Charlotte went through a phase where she was obsessed with pearls, and Mr. Jones took notice. So what did he do? He ordered oysters, brought them over, and they cut the pearls out together. Who does that?

He made Charlotte breakfast on her first day of fifth grade and even asked if he could join us in bringing her to school. It was a big day for us. We had traditions in place, and his efforts felt admirable. He often suggested ways for us to spend time together, always including my daughter, which I especially appreciated—no one else had ever seemed worthy of knowing her. He showed a genuine interest in what mattered to both of us. When she had cheerleading practice, he came to support us—something her own father rarely did.

In those early days, recognizing him as a narcissist felt impossible. Narcissists are masters of disguise—attractive, charismatic, and caring. They know exactly how to present themselves in a way that makes you feel safe, wanted, and secure. I didn't recognize the signs until it was too late. By then, I found myself asking, *What's wrong with me?*

Understanding the signs of narcissistic abuse is crucial to breaking free from its grip. Some of the most common red flags include belittling, gaslighting, manipulation, and a lack of empathy. Narcissists are also skilled at isolating you from your support system, making you question your own reality. Looking back, I now see the patterns that were there from the beginning.

Charm and Charisma

Narcissists often make an unforgettable first impression. They're captivating, and their charm can easily blind you to the red flags. I remember how he hugged me on our first date—he may have even asked for permission first. When he leaned in to kiss me, he asked. I thought, Is this what gentlemen do? It felt so respectful. I missed the subtle manipulations beneath the surface.

Love-Bombing

Love-bombing involves showering their target with excessive attention, affection, and gifts to create an emotional bond. At the time, it all seemed so subtle. Despite his long commute and demanding work hours, he drove to see me almost daily—even before I lost my driver's license. He casually offered hotel stays and gifted us everything from shoes and kitchen appliances to electronics and even small pets. Things that seemed thoughtful were really just tools of control.

Manipulation

Narcissists are expert manipulators. Mr. Jones always found a way to criticize my friends and family, implying they weren't trustworthy or reliable. Over time, he convinced me that my only constant was him.

Projection

Narcissists often project their own flaws and insecurities onto you. Looking back, I can't believe I didn't see it sooner. His early stories of pain and loneliness played on my sympathies, making me want to help him—but that vulnerability was just a façade.

Idealization and Devaluation Cycle

At first, narcissists put you on a pedestal, making you feel adored. But over time, they begin to belittle and devalue you. I remember when he asked me, "How many sexual partners have you had?" I thought honesty was essential, so I told him the truth. To him, my higher number meant I was an untrustworthy, cheating whore. From that moment on, he used my past as a weapon, accusing me of infidelity—mainly because I worked from home and had the flexibility and freedom to have someone over. Despite our constant contact, he accused me regularly.

Triangular Relationships

Narcissists create chaos by drawing other people into the relationship dynamic. He isolated me from friends and family, but more devastatingly, he drove a wedge between me and my daughter. Charlotte and I had always been close, strong in our mother-daughter bond, but he slowly turned us against each other. He became the mediator in our arguments—the one she would turn to when we fought. And I let it happen.

— • • • —

Charlotte started going to him whenever we argued, venting about me—her mom, teacher, and principal—all while reporting any time she saw me talking to another man. Our once-healthy relationship was in shambles.

Mr. Jones was inconsistent. A straight-up liar, really, but I didn't see it clearly back then. Once, he went to his sister's wedding in Jamaica. We had just broken up before his trip, and during that time, I made a mistake. I relapsed. I tried to numb the pain or escape the anger in the only ways I knew how—a few bumps of coke and I got two tattoos that day, marking my skin as if that could somehow release what was breaking inside me. Even so, we still spoke while he was away, and when he returned, everything seemed fine.

Months later, I found out his ex-girlfriend had been there with him. When I confronted him, he denied they were together, claiming his family had invited her. I was furious. *Are you fucking kidding me?*

Why did it take me so long to see the red flags? Or did I refuse to accept them? Narcissists are experts at keeping you in the dark. They gaslight you, distort your reality, and make it hard to trust your instincts. You start questioning everything—even your own sanity.

By fall 2019, I finally considered moving on. When he found out, he rushed home from a work trip to confront me. I was honest with him again. He lost his mind. Yelling, screaming, throwing things. At one point, he flung my phone across the table, sending hot candle wax splattering all over my face, arms, and eyes. Then, as his rage subsided, he blamed me.

I had ruined everything, he said. I had destroyed his plans to propose on my birthday the following month. He held that guilt over me for a long time, waving around a lease for an apartment he supposedly secured for us in Orange County, flashing a receipt for a ring he claimed he had bought. He even said he had planned to propose in Seattle, his favorite place.

Hoodwinked. *Now, I can't help but wonder—was any of it real? Or was it just another layer of his deception?*

We attempted couples therapy, but it went nowhere. We never got past our first session because he refused to discuss his upbringing or family issues. I should have seen the red flags. *Why didn't I recognize the signs sooner? Why did I believe he was the one?* I was so angry with myself—for being vulnerable, for letting him into our lives, for trusting him.

If you have been manipulated, deceived, or abused, know this: You are not alone. And it is not your fault. You are not weak or naïve—you believed you were in love. Healing starts with reflection, seeking support from trusted friends or professionals, and setting boundaries. You deserve better. You are worthy.

Find it funny you just can't apologize
Egotistic, narcissistic, love your own lies
See you the reason why strong women fucked up
Why they say it's a man's world, see you the reason for Trump
You the reason, we overlooked, underpaid, under booked, under shame
If you look, I don't speak, then I'm called out my name
I am flawed, I am pained, never yours, I remained
— Kendrick Lamar & Taylour Paige, We Cry Together,
Mr. Morale & The Big Steppers

That day was suffocating—filled with overwhelming fear, frustration, and disturbing flashbacks. It brought memories of past toxicity and abuse rushing back, as if I had never escaped that world.

But he relished his ability to control and manipulate me, taking cruel pleasure in exploiting my vulnerability and past trauma.

"Get in the fucking car, Aisa!"

His command was disturbingly familiar. I complied. And he drove off recklessly, with no clear destination. Hard stops. Abrupt turns. Running red lights.

He pulled up to the QVC warehouse near my apartment, parked, and ordered me to open his glove compartment.

My body tensed. My breath caught in my throat as I struggled to process what was happening. *Was I in danger? Would he actually harm me?*

Then—his voice again. Cold. Controlled. "Get the gun."

My hands trembled as I reached into the glove compartment. His threats blurred into aggressive gibberish, his words twisting into something I couldn't fully grasp.

The audacity of this man—trying to intimidate me. Threaten me. Control me. *How had I allowed anyone to speak to me like this again?*

I got out of the car and started rushing home, my heart pounding with panic and distress. But Mr. Jones wasn't done. He drove up beside me and yelled, "Get back in the fucking car, Aisa!"

I ignored him, pushing forward. But as I made it halfway to the stoplight, he suddenly blocked my path, parking his car directly in front of me.

Reluctantly, I returned to the car. I don't remember much of what was said after that. But before letting me out, he reached into the glove compartment, pulled out a bullet, and handed it to me—as if to remind me that he had spared my life.

He wanted me to believe that no matter what happened, no matter if I moved on, I would always need him. That he would always be watching.

I kept that bullet. But not as a symbol of his control. I kept it as a reminder—of the power I refused to give away again. Of the resentment that still lingers when I think back on those *darkest* days. I haven't spoken to him since. *Thank you, Lord.*

The Reality of Narcissistic Abuse

Narcissistic abuse is more common than many realize. Studies show that approximately 1 in 4 women and 1 in 9 men experience physical violence, emotional abuse, or stalking by a narcissistic partner or family member. A survey further revealed that 72% of respondents had faced narcissistic abuse at some point in their lives.

Recovering from such a relationship takes time, self-compassion, and professional support. Prioritizing your mental and emotional well-being is crucial. Therapy, counseling, and support groups specializing in narcissistic and emotional abuse can help survivors rebuild their self-worth and autonomy.

Establishing healthy boundaries, practicing self-care, and engaging in activities that promote personal growth are essential steps in reclaiming yourself. Breaking free from a narcissistic relationship and overcoming trauma bonding requires immense strength and courage.

Navigating these complex dynamics can feel overwhelming and discouraging, but by recognizing the red flags, seeking support, and prioritizing your healing, you can reclaim your life and move toward a future filled with hope and possibility.

You Are Not Alone

There is a supportive community ready to stand by you. Every step you take—no matter how small—brings you closer to the freedom and peace you deserve.

"We have freedom now, because Christ made us free. So stand strong in that freedom. Don't go back into slavery again."

Galatians 5:1 ERV

AWAKEN & *Reflect*

Embarking on a journey of healing and
self-discovery after experiencing any form
of abuse is a courageous endeavor.
I will give myself grace to heal at my own pace.

AWARENESS:

How have my past experiences with toxic patterns
influenced my self-perception and the boundaries
I establish in relationships?

_____

_____

_____

_____

_____

_____

_____

_____

_____

_____

_____

_____

_____

_____

_____

_____

_____

_____

_____

WORK IT:

How can I reframe negative beliefs I hold about myself due to the relational trauma to reflect the truth about my identity and self-worth?

_____

_____

_____

_____

_____

_____

_____

_____

_____

_____

_____

_____

_____

_____

_____

_____

_____

_____

_____

_____

ALIGNMENT:

Which of my core values and passions may have
been suppressed during the seasons of unhealthy
dynamics, and how can I realign with them now?

_____

_____

_____

_____

_____

_____

_____

_____

_____

_____

_____

_____

_____

_____

_____

_____

_____

_____

_____

KNOWLEDGE:

What have I learned about the dynamics of
emotionally damaging relationships that can
empower me moving forward?

_____

_____

_____

_____

_____

_____

_____

_____

_____

_____

_____

_____

_____

_____

_____

_____

_____

_____

EMBRACE:

What aspects of my journey can I embrace as evidence of my resilience and strength?

_____

_____

_____

_____

_____

_____

_____

_____

_____

_____

_____

_____

_____

_____

_____

_____

_____

_____

NAVIGATE:

How can I navigate future relationships to ensure they are healthy and mutually respectful?

_____

_____

_____

_____

_____

_____

_____

_____

_____

_____

_____

_____

_____

_____

_____

_____

_____

"THE LORD IS CLOSE TO THE BROKENHEARTED AND
SAVES THOSE WHO ARE CRUSHED IN SPIRIT."
— PSALM 34:18

CHAPTER EIGHT

AWAKEN

It was the Monday after Thanksgiving, and I had finally reached the point where I was ready to let go of Mr. Jones completely. The lies, broken promises, and his last-minute cancellation of plans with Charlotte were too much. That was my breaking point.

This decision—to shut the door on all things Mr. Jones—marked both my darkest days and the beginning of a beautiful awakening.

The unraveling began with a transformational massage by a local therapist I had been following on Instagram. I walked into the session unknowingly carrying the weight of trapped trauma in my back and hips, along with the stress and pain in my shoulders that I had been holding onto for so long.

Then, something profound happened. During the massage, I surrendered to God. In that moment of yielding, I felt my burdens begin to lift. The sound bath, the vibrations, the pressure, and the movement all reflected a deeper spiritual release within me.

The therapist guided my breathwork, instructing me to grunt, moan, and release—not just sound, but tension. For the first time, I understood what it meant to find a safe healing space—physically, spiritually, and emotionally. I had never experienced anything like it before.

After the session, the therapist and I delved into a conversation about microdosing psychedelic mushrooms. I confided that I had experimented with it before, but my experience had been limited—just a few tears, heightened emotions, nothing transformational.

He offered a fresh perspective. "Microdosing isn't just about altering perception or chasing a high," he explained. "It's about forging new neural pathways, rewiring thought patterns, and shifting emotional responses at the core."

His words stayed with me. Intrigued, I decided to take a psilocybin capsule after he left, open to discovering where this new understanding might lead me.

Psilocybin is far more than a "magic mushroom." It's a powerful tool for psychological and emotional healing. It promotes neuroplasticity, allowing the brain to form new connections and rewire outdated thought patterns. This process enhances cognitive flexibility, emotional regulation, and overall well-being. Many use it to confront past traumas, break free from deep-seated emotional cycles, and embark on a journey of radical self-acceptance and growth.

That night, I picked up a book I had started but never finished, *The Man God Has for You* by Stephen Labossiere. As I read, something shifted. Tears welled up in my eyes. Then, they poured.

A flood of negative self-talk consumed me. *How could I*

have been so naïve? Why did I allow myself to be so vulnerable to Mr. Jones?

But as the tears subsided, another voice emerged—the voice of my massage therapist. His words echoed in my mind.

"You have the power to reshape your inner narrative."

For the first time, I chose to challenge the lies I had been telling myself. I spoke back to the self-destructive thoughts, confronting them with truth. I had to name it to reframe it. I realized that healing wasn't just about letting go—it was about rewriting the story I told myself about who I was.

I could forge new neural pathways. I could transform my thinking. I could change my life.

Finally, I cried out to God, asking Him to bless me with my Boaz. I prayed that if Mr. Jones wasn't the one, God would make it unmistakably clear and remove him from our lives. As Pastor Bianca from Revere Church says, "Bless and release!"

Later that week, my mentor Andrea and I set up our first vendor table, promoting Club Nirvana's premier cannabis products at a pop-up event in downtown Los Angeles. The energy was electric—vendors lined the venue, music vibrated through the air, and I wandered through the space, with a blunt in hand, networking and browsing the booths.

That's when I met Michael. *Could he be my Boaz?*

I wouldn't make the connection until much later, but something about him stood out instantly—his energy, the depth in his gaze, the way he carried himself. And, of course, the life-changing infused iced coffee he introduced me to. It felt like a new chapter was quietly unfolding in the background, even as I remained deeply immersed in my healing journey.

On the drive home, Andrea and I celebrated the night's success—good vibes, strong sales, and fire flower. But suddenly, a wave of nausea crept up my throat. Before I knew it, I was projectile vomiting uncontrollably.

Thankfully, Andrea, always prepared, handed me a few plastic grocery bags to contain the mess. The car reeked of weed and vomit, but instead of being horrified, we burst into uncontrollable laughter—like two carefree teenage girls munching on elotes and Hot Cheetos, lost on the wrong freeway, but somehow still filled with so much joy.

For nearly a month after that night, every car ride triggered my body's need to purge. I knew about purging in a psychedelic sense—how, during a psilocybin experience, vomiting, diarrhea, sweating, or tears could symbolize a cathartic release of negative energies, emotions, and toxins. It's uncomfortable, yes. But it's also radically cleansing.

Was this my body's way of ridding itself of all things Mr. Jones and every other toxic influence I had carried for too long? I believe it was. It was the beginning of a much-needed process of letting go.

As I distanced myself from Mr. Jones, everything began to shift. Whether it was the awakening sparked by psilocybin or simply the relief of escaping his narcissistic grip, I wasn't sure. What I did know was that he noticed—and he made it clear that moving on from him would be a mistake. One I'd regret.

He tried to intimidate me, claiming that he or his people were watching me, even when I was by the pool in my gated community. He allegedly sent someone to my apartment on several occasions—a calculated reminder of his presence. A way to keep me nervous and afraid.

Then came the last time he showed up at my apartment. His rage was uncontrollable as our arguing continued. He kicked my bed frame until it broke, then grabbed me and threw me onto the bed—again and again. Each time, his grip felt stronger, tighter, more relentless.

I managed to pull myself up and make my way to the garage—I had a delivery arriving. He rushed after me.

Just as I stepped out of the elevator, Charlotte was arriving home with her friend. She saw everything. The yelling. The tension between us. I told them both to go upstairs.

What officially set him off? Jealousy? Suspicion? Some delusional paranoia? I'll never know.

Then, in a flash of anger, he snatched the bottle of iced coffee from my hands and hurled it at me. Cold, sticky coffee soaked my clothes and dripped through my hair, but I barely had time to process it all.

Neighbors passed by, their eyes filled with curiosity, concern—or maybe judgement.

His obsessive need for control was suffocating. *Who was this man? This rage? This sudden, desperate need for dominance?*

My *darkest* day with Mr. Jones was apparently the wake-up call I needed to begin healing—mentally, emotionally, and physically. *Thank you, Lord.*

——————— • • • ———————

During this tumultuous period in my life, I was blessed to have crossed paths with a new Michael—though at the time, we were just getting to know each other. Mike gave me the best advice I didn't even realize I needed.

With a straightforwardness that caught me off guard,

he pointed out something I hadn't fully confronted: he said I had some unresolved issues I needed to handle, particularly concerning my previous relationship.

At first, I was taken aback, and perhaps even slightly offended. How could someone who barely knew me presume to tell me what I needed to do?

But over time, I realized that his words were one of the kindest gifts anyone could have given me. Mike led with love, compassion, and understanding, giving me the space and support I needed to heal—body, mind, and spirit.

So, I dedicated myself to the process. Every day. Sunshine or raindrops. I moved my body—doing exercises in the pool and jacuzzi, often breaking down in tears, releasing emotions I had buried for far too long. My ugly Kim K. cry made regular appearances as I listened to the audiobook, *Boundaries: When to Say Yes, How to Say No to Take Control of Your Life*, by Dr. Henry Cloud and Dr. John Townsend on Audible, on repeat.

I decided to do the work to heal. I was determined to face all the pain, sadness, and anger head-on—to process it and move forward, not just push it aside.

There would be no more "fuck it" attitude! No alternative substances. No distractions. No numbing my emotions. Nothing to turn to for escape or comfort. I was committed to doing the work, to healing, to reclaiming all parts of myself so I could finally become whole. I believed that I could do this. And so I did.

Then Jesus said, "Come to me, all of you who are weary and carry heavy burdens, and I will give you rest."

Matthew 11:28 NLT

AWAKEN & *Reflect*

Awakening isn't just about one defining moment—it can come in unexpected ways, through challenges, breakthroughs, or intentional practices. Sometimes, awakening happens in our darkest days, showing us the light that was there all along.

AWARENESS:

Have you ever experienced a moment where
everything suddenly became clearer? What sparked
that awakening?

_____

_____

_____

_____

_____

_____

_____

_____

_____

_____

_____

_____

_____

_____

_____

_____

_____

_____

WORK IT:

What intentional practices—whether physical,
emotional, or spiritual—can help you deepen your
awakening and continue growing?

_____

_____

_____

_____

_____

_____

_____

_____

_____

_____

_____

_____

_____

_____

_____

_____

_____

ALIGNMENT:

When faced with both light and darkness at the same time, how can you shift your perspective to see the good that is happening?

_____

_____

_____

_____

_____

_____

_____

_____

_____

_____

_____

_____

_____

_____

_____

_____

_____

_____

_____

_____

KNOWLEDGE:

What have past awakenings taught you
about your resilience, your ability to heal,
or the power of perception?

_____

_____

_____

_____

_____

_____

_____

_____

_____

_____

_____

_____

_____

_____

_____

_____

_____

_____

_____

_____

_____

_____

_____

_____

EMBRACE:

How can you fully accept this season of
transformation without resistance or fear?

_____

_____

_____

_____

_____

_____

_____

_____

_____

_____

_____

_____

_____

_____

_____

_____

_____

_____

NAVIGATE:

What is one conscious step you can take today to
honor this awakening and move forward
with intention?

_____

_____

_____

_____

_____

_____

_____

_____

_____

_____

_____

_____

_____

_____

_____

_____

"WAKE UP, SLEEPER, RISE FROM THE DEAD,
AND CHRIST WILL SHINE ON YOU."
— EPHESIANS 5:14

CHAPTER NINE

COUNT IT ALL JOY

J oy is often seen as a distant reward, something waiting for us at the end of the darkest tunnels. But what if joy isn't just found after the struggle—what if it can be found within it?

What if every setback isn't an obstacle, but a divinely arranged opportunity for growth? As we explore the valleys I've walked through and the mountains I've climbed, you'll discover how, with a grateful heart, even the toughest terrain—whether I was using a walking cane or not—revealed the undeniable hand of my Creator. Every low point, every peak, didn't just test my resilience. They nudged me forward, shaping me into who I was always meant to be.

This turning point in my healing journey began with an observant physical therapist, whose keen listening skills and invaluable feedback led to a life-saving revelation. Initially, I sought treatment for neck issues, but I also voiced concerns about my lower back to her, which I felt was a more critical problem. During one session, I mentioned numbness in my inner thigh, suspecting it was related to sciatica.

She didn't hesitate. "That could be a sign of cauda equina compression," she warned. "It's serious and can lead to paralysis from the waist down. If you experience incontinence or loss of sensation, you need to go to the emergency room immediately."

I listened, but I wasn't too worried—until a few weeks later. One morning, I thought I had leaked urine without any apparent reason. No hysterical laughing, no smoker's cough. Just ... leaked.

I remembered what my therapist had said. Worried about the possibility of cauda equina compression, my brother dropped me off at the emergency room of San Antonio Regional Hospital. Little did I know that my life was about to change drastically yet again.

The doctor reviewed my scans and delivered the news: I had herniated discs and bulges in my L4 and L5, compressing the nerves in my cauda equina region. I needed emergency spinal surgery—and just like that, a laminectomy and microdiscectomy was scheduled for the very next morning.

Wait, what? No second opinions? No time for a deep-dive Google search?

What happened to consulting with me first—showing me X-rays like they do on TV? *Grey's Anatomy, House— where was my dramatic diagnostic moment? Where was my opportunity to decide what happens next?*

I barely had time to process it before the fear and anxiety hit. I made a quick call to my cousin Maria, needing to hear a familiar voice before everything became too overwhelming.

Then, I had a brief emotional breakdown.

Fortunately, the surgery went smoothly, without complications, but the recovery process was far more challenging than I expected. I distinctly remember accidentally dropping a water bottle on the floor and crying—not because of the bottle, but at my inability to pick it up.

The small incision above my tailbone, barely noticeable, is a constant reminder that I am not my old self. Pain that had once been localized in my back now spread to my hips, accompanied by weakness and numbness in my hamstrings and the sides of my legs.

Navigating the healthcare system during my recovery was exhausting, as it is for many other patients. I faced long wait times for follow-up appointments, struggled to find specialists who understood my conditions, and spent endless hours coordinating between multiple healthcare providers. Despite advancements in medical technology, I often felt lost in the system, fighting to get the proper care and support I needed.

Then came the insurance battles. Denials, delays, and confusing policies left me frustrated and uncertain about coverage for my treatments. I spent countless hours on the phone with insurance representatives, advocating for treatments and tests I should have automatically qualified for. It was disheartening—I should have been focusing on recovery, not fighting bureaucracy. Even when I secured coverage, policy limitations forced me to settle for less effective treatments, making the entire process even more frustrating.

The stigma surrounding cannabis only added to my already complicated situation. Despite its legal status in California, cannabis is still federally illegal for medical and adult recreational use, meaning insurance wouldn't cover it as legitimate treatment. Instead, I was often left with medications and options that weren't as effective, simply because of the outdated policies and red tape. More muscles relaxers, more pain pills, and more steroid injections.

I realized the importance of seeking external support and advocacy to overcome these obstacles. I could complain, feel discouraged, or take action. I chose the latter.

I reached out to organizations like Global Genes, Rare Across America, Rare Compassion Program, and the Hypersomnia Foundation. They provided resources, guidance, and support, helping me understand my rights as a patient, connect with others facing similar challenges, and navigate the complexities of the healthcare system. Their assistance and advocacy was invaluable, offering clarity in moments of confusion, hopelessness, and frustration.

My journey through the healthcare system highlighted the pressing need for reform. It became evident that the system was inherently flawed, with significant access and coverage barriers. I became passionate about advocating for change, supporting initiatives to improve patient care, reduce insurance complexities, and enhance support systems for individuals facing health challenges.

Yet, despite my determination and advocacy, the weight of chronic pain and medication side effects drained my mental and emotional well-being.

There were nights when I found myself struggling with thoughts of suicidal ideation—not just because of the unbearable physical pain, but because of how it eroded my sense of self and disrupted my daily life. When you spend more time managing your pain and long list of prescriptions than actually living, everything begins to spiral downward.

Losing the ability to drive and the independence that came with it, struggling to make my bed each morning, even being unable to write my daily agenda due to an unsteady hand—all of these were constant reminders of the person I used to be. And the deep grief of losing that version of myself was something I hadn't fully processed.

Living with invisible illnesses like idiopathic hypersomnia and cauda equina syndrome brought challenges that were hard to explain to others. The exhaustion, memory lapses, and lack of concentration made every day a battle. But even worse? The lack of understanding from medical professionals, which only deepened my frustration.

Walking with a cane, wearing a back brace when needed, and spending hours in water therapy became part of my reality. Yet, I still felt the crushing pressure to maintain the "independent supermom" persona—an image that weighed heavily on me, irritating my spirit because it symbolized all I had to face alone.

Then, things began to shift.

I turned to cannabis with intention—not just for relief, but for true medicinal healing. In December 2021, at a pop-up night market, I discovered an iced coffee infused with full-spectrum cannabis extract. By then, I had already heard of RSO (Rick Simpson Oil) from the documentary *Weed the People*, which had first sparked my interest in plant medicine.

"OMFG, this is amazing!"

Not only did it taste delicious, but more importantly, I loved how I felt. This wasn't the dazed and confused high most people associate with cannabis. This was something entirely different—a feeling of balance, homeostasis, focus, and energy, with a good sprinkle of creativity. It was similar to how I felt when the Adderall finally kicked in, but with none of the withdrawal symptoms or side effects. Wow.

There is such a massive misconception that cannabis makes everyone lazy or sleepy; this infused coffee and creamer provided an overall full body sense of healing and wellness in ways I hadn't fully understood yet. A few days later, I ordered more.

At that time, I was taking twelve prescriptions daily. Now, I drink a 12-ounce cup of coffee with infused French vanilla creamer every morning. Absolutely no more Adderall, Vyvanse, Ritalin, Nuvigil, or Provigil!

Cannabis also helps me move, walk, and function better. It works as a pre-workout boost, pain reliever, and recovery aid. Some days, I can move and walk better than others, but cannabis as a whole has provided me with healing that neither Gabapentin, Tramadol, Hydrocodone, Norco, or Baclofen ever could.

Through it all, I have finally understood what it means to count it all joy. This joy isn't about being happy despite suffering, it's about recognizing that every trial, every hardship, every set back is part of a larger, divine plan for growth and healing.

The hurt, the hang-ups, and the habits that once held me back? They were never meant to break me. They were meant to become stepping stones on my path to wholeness.

There were moments when I felt utterly broken, unsure of how to move forward. But looking back, I now see that those moments were not the end. They were the beginning of a new chapter in my life. God was at work amid my pain, shaping me into who I am today.

Despite everything, I refused to be defined by my limitations and circumstances. I realized that my experiences were not meant to be kept hidden, buried in shame. They were meant to be shared—to inspire, to comfort, to uplift those who are brokenhearted. By sharing our stories, we empower both ourselves and others to find strength, hope, and joy even in the midst of adversity.

As we close this chapter, I hope you see that joy isn't merely the reward waiting for us at the end of our trials. Joy is the light we can choose to see, even in our darkest moments. The valleys and mountains of life are not random. They are divinely designed to shape us, to draw us closer to our purpose, and reveal the strength we didn't know we had.

Every challenge is a chapter in the story of our becoming—a testament to the faithfulness of a Creator who lovingly guides us through every tear and triumph. May you walk away with the courage to *count it all joy*, knowing that each step you take—whether through shadows or sunlight—is leading you to the person you are meant to be.

"Rejoice in the Lord always: and again I say, Rejoice. Let your moderation be known unto all men. The Lord is at hand. Be careful for nothing; but in every thing by prayer and supplication with thanksgiving let your requests be made known unto God."

Philippians 4:4-6 KJV

AWAKEN & *Reflect*

Finding joy in the midst of hardship isn't about
pretending everything is okay—it's about recognizing
that even in our struggles, there is purpose.

AWARENESS:

Think of a time when life took an unexpected turn.
How did that experience change your perspective?

_____

_____

_____

_____

_____

_____

_____

_____

_____

_____

_____

_____

_____

_____

_____

_____

_____

_____

WORK IT:

The way we speak to ourselves matters.
Name a limiting belief you've held onto
and reframe it with truth.

(Example: "I am broken" ↠ "I am learning, healing, and growing.")

_____

_____

_____

_____

_____

_____

_____

_____

_____

_____

_____

_____

_____

_____

_____

_____

_____

_____

ALIGNMENT:

What helps you stay grounded and find peace
during difficult seasons? How can you make
space for more of that in your life?

_____

_____

_____

_____

_____

_____

_____

_____

_____

_____

_____

_____

_____

_____

_____

_____

_____

_____

_____

_____

_____

_____

KNOWLEDGE:

What is one lesson a challenging time has taught you about your strength and resilience?

_____

_____

_____

_____

_____

_____

_____

_____

_____

_____

_____

_____

_____

_____

_____

_____

_____

_____

EMBRACE:

Instead of resisting struggle, what would it look like to embrace it as part of your journey?

_____

_____

_____

_____

_____

_____

_____

_____

_____

_____

_____

_____

_____

_____

_____

_____

_____

_____

_____

_____

NAVIGATE:

What is one step you can take today to move forward
with joy, even in uncertainty?

_____

_____

_____

_____

_____

_____

_____

_____

_____

_____

_____

_____

_____

_____

_____

_____

"CONSIDER IT PURE JOY, MY BROTHERS AND SISTERS, WHENEVER
YOU FACE TRIALS OF MANY KINDS, BECAUSE YOU KNOW THAT
THE TESTING OF YOUR FAITH PRODUCES PERSEVERANCE."
— JAMES 1:2-3

CHAPTER TEN

HEALING

As someone who has suffered from idiopathic hypersomnia nearly my entire life but has struggled more so in the past seven years, I often questioned why God would keep me in a state of perpetual slumber. Inspired by *The Body Keeps the Score* by Bessel van der Kolk—which I also listened to on repeat during my water exercises—I began exploring the connection between dissociation as a form of protection and the divine purpose behind my prolonged sleep.

In *The Body Keeps the Score*, van der Kolk explains that dissociation is a defense mechanism the brain uses to cope with overwhelming or traumatic experiences. It creates a sense of detachment from oneself, one's emotions, or the surrounding environment—a survival strategy that can leave people feeling disconnected from reality and protected from its full impact. Paralysis, too, is a response to trauma, often manifesting when the body's stress response system becomes overwhelmed.

Dr. Gabor Maté, author of *When the Body Says No: The Cost of Hidden Stress*, delves into how trauma and stress leave lasting imprints on both the body and the mind. Maté emphasizes that unresolved trauma often manifests in chronic conditions and illnesses, signaling that the body is trying to communicate something deeper.

He also has a unique perspective on addiction, viewing it not as a failure of willpower or a moral flaw but as a coping mechanism for deep, unresolved pain. According to Maté, addiction is a form of self-soothing—whether through substances, behaviors, or relationships—that people use to numb the emotional wounds left by trauma.

This perspective resonated deeply with me. Looking back on the years I spent battling addiction—turning to drugs, unhealthy relationships, and avoidance—I realize now that it wasn't just about seeking pleasure or escape. I was trying to numb the emotional pain that had been lingering in my body for so long.

The trauma I had carried throughout my life manifested in addiction or illness, and it was only by facing that trauma directly that I began to heal. Maté's work helped me understand that the roots of my addiction weren't the substances or behaviors themselves, but the unresolved pain, anger, grief, fear, and shame I hadn't fully processed.

Could it be a mere coincidence that I suffer from a rare neurological disorder that leaves me excessively sleepy and trapped in an uncontrollable, unexpected brain fog with sleep drunkenness? Or that I endured paralysis and numbness in my lower back down my legs from cauda equina compression due to herniated discs in my spine? Or that I have overcome addiction, a laminectomy, microdiscectomy, and a spinal fusion all before hitting forty years old? I now know that coincidences do not exist in God's Kingdom, so I wondered, *Why, God, why?! For what?*

Perhaps my hypersomnia was God's way of forcing me to slow down and smell the roses. Maybe it was His way of making me stop buying into the world's false narrative of the "hustle and grind" culture. I was always saying yes to everyone, spreading myself too thin, and then resenting myself and those I had said yes to. My body and spirit were crying out for rest, and God, in His wisdom, granted me that through hypersomnia. Maybe this sleep wasn't just a burden—it was a divine intervention, a way of ensuring that I took the time to be still and trust in Him, to recalibrate my life according to His purpose rather than the relentless demands of the world.

Psalm 127:2 says, "It is vain for you to rise up early, to sit up late, to eat the bread of sorrows: for so he giveth his beloved sleep." This verse suggests that God grants sleep as a gift to those who trust in Him, indicating peace and security.

As I reflected on this, I realized that my hypersomnia might be more than just a medical condition or the devastating cause of losing my driver's license—it could be a protective mechanism, a way for my body and mind to grieve and process trauma while resting safely in God's embrace.

Perhaps it was His way of showing me to trust Him with my health, daughter, home, finances, and relationships. I felt like Job in the Bible. But God is faithful! He made a covenant with me, shared His promises and provision, and began preparing me for what He had already set aside for me. Although, I didn't recognize that at the time.

Exploring the connection between dissociation and

idiopathic hypersomnia provides a unique perspective on the concept of sleep and rest. While not directly related to these conditions, the biblical narratives of Abraham and Adam's deep sleep highlight themes of trust, surrender, and divine intervention. By holistically approaching sleep and its related conditions, we can incorporate scientific research, psychological insights, and spiritual contemplation into our understanding.

This journey has taught me that healing requires more than just physical recovery. It's about emotional, mental, and spiritual transformation, too. Exploring the relationship between trauma, dissociation, and sleep through a holistic lens—blending science, psychology, and faith—has helped me embrace the peace that only God can provide.

Brainspotting

I can't talk about healing without mentioning brainspotting. Developed by Dr. David Grand, it's a therapeutic approach designed to help people process unresolved trauma by identifying "brain spots" linked to emotional pain.

Praise God that my therapist at the time became certified in brainspotting just when I needed it.

During a session, my therapist would guide me to focus on a brain spot as she moved her wand. Sometimes, I would get anxious, unsure of what I was supposed to feel. But as my attention zeroed in on these specific areas, my body would react. I could feel sensations in my throat, chest, and legs. The energy would start to move, my breathing would shift, and my body would tense.

Then, the tears would come—uncontrollable but profoundly healing. I couldn't pinpoint exactly why I cried, but something inside was being released.

I've had four brainspotting sessions, each one opening a different door, peeling away another layer of the trauma I've carried. It's not just magic—it's neuroscience at work, accessing the limbic system, the part of the brain responsible for emotion. Brainspotting has helped me process and release the memories and feelings I couldn't before, and I've noticed the healing in every aspect of my life.

In one session, I decided to focus on sex. I didn't know what I needed to address or uncover, but what happened during that session blew my mind. It was like a revelation: I have a clean slate now—a new beginning. My past sexual experiences, mistakes, or desires don't define me anymore. My sexual being is just a part of who I am, not the sum of my identity. I don't need to carry shame about it anymore.

Through these sessions, I've begun to understand that my past trauma doesn't define my perspective on sex today. Where I once felt numb, I also made impulsive, provocative, and sometimes promiscuous decisions, projecting my pain in multiple ways.

Now, I am fully present—physically, mentally, emotionally, and spiritually. I have discovered who I am. First, I experienced God's agape love, and through that love, I found the one my soul desires.

With Mike, I feel truly seen. He respects me, loves me, inspires me, understands me, and lifts me up. God showed me how He loves me and then blessed me with Mike to demonstrate what love looks like in the flesh. It's overwhelming at times, almost too good to be true. Sometimes, I worry that if I enjoy it too much, it might be taken from me. *Why do I struggle to see it any other way?*

Brainspotting isn't just about trauma—it can also help unlock peak performance. It clears emotional blocks, assisting people to break through barriers in all areas of life, even in completing long-overdue memoirs.

The Deep Healing

Healing, I've come to realize, isn't just about overcoming physical pain or trauma. It's a holistic process that transforms and renews your mind, body, and soul. It requires a deliberate and holistic approach, embracing various modalities that work together to restore balance and wholeness. This process can manifest in different ways: through emotional breakthroughs, physical recovery, spiritual enlightenment, or a combination of all three. To become truly whole, one must navigate through a series of stages, each offering unique insights and opportunities for growth.

In July 2023, I tuned into an online sermon by Pastor Bianca from Revere Church titled, "How am I, really? Do you want to be made well?" Although I'd been reading devotionals for years, I hadn't truly immersed myself in the Word. But when Pastor B recounted the story of the paralytic man by the Pool of Bethesda, who made excuses for why he couldn't reach the healing waters, something clicked.

She described how the paralytic man, lying there for thirty-eight years, gave Jesus all kinds of excuses about why he hadn't been able to reach the healing waters—how no one had carried him there, how he had tried but always fallen short as others made it to the water first (John 5:7). And then, Pastor B posed the same question that Jesus asked him: "Do you want to be made well?"

At that moment, I wept.

Those words pierced my heart because I knew they were meant for me. I was that man by the pool, feeling trapped by my circumstances, hurt from the lack of support, longing for healing but uncertain how to reach it. It was as if Jesus was speaking directly to me, asking if I was ready to stop waiting, take up my mat, and walk.

I wanted to become whole! I decided to take action. That moment led me to seek new doctors and I went to Cedars-Sinai Hospital in Beverly Hills for a second opinion. In January 2024, I had my second back surgery, an anterior spinal fusion. Their level of care was an absolute blessing, from the initial consultation with pain management and neurosurgery to my one-year post-op appointment. They saw me—really saw me—and prioritized my healing and recovery. But the transformation wasn't just physical. God was working on my heart, too. He wasn't just healing my spine but rebuilding me from the inside out. He was rebuilding my foundation.

Then came the recovery period. As much as I thought I was prepared this time around for my surgery and recovery, I was wrong. I stocked up on all the helpful tools—the shower handles, a walker, and a grabber. I made transportation arrangements for Charlotte with my mom and my brother. I met with my attorney, finalized my living trust, and revisited the difficult decisions I had to make for myself and my daughter before facing this intimidating and complex procedure. Yet, I soon realized that no amount of preparation could fully equip me for what was to come. No one truly prepares you for these moments. Throughout this journey, I felt as though I had to do it all alone, with no one to guide me or understand what I was going through. But during these challenging times, I recognized just how much my Heavenly Father was with me every step of the way.

What I especially didn't anticipate, however, was the emotional rollercoaster that followed. I had expected the physical pain and the challenges of limited mobility, but I hadn't considered the impact it would have on my emotional and mental state. When I asked God to make me whole, I never imagined He would do so in the way that He did. *But isn't that always the case?*

I began to experience a deep and meaningful shift as if He was healing me from within, not just mending the fractures in my spine but realigning the very core of my being. Literally and figuratively. It was as though the healing wasn't just physical—it was a rebuilding of my foundation by discovering who I am through Him. Layer by layer, restoring not only my body but also the resilience of my spirit. He was healing my heart, tearing out the old, and renewing my mind, body, and soul. It was as if He was preparing me for all the promises He had in store for me.

Through this process, God not only restored my physical health by healing the scars on my tummy and the two new ones on my back, but He also redeemed relationships I didn't even know I needed or desired. After years of conflict and tension, He brought my stepdad and me closer than ever before. He taught me to accept friends, family, and colleagues as they are, to grieve the relationships I once hoped for or held on to for too long, and to love people from a distance when necessary.

Navigating these complexities with grace has drawn me closer to Him, deepening my understanding of His love for me. Most importantly, He has shown me how to love myself and others in the way I was designed to.

As you read this, I hope you feel inspired to embrace your own journey of healing. Trust that the process, however unexpected, will bring you closer to the wholeness you seek. Allow yourself to be transformed, to love deeply, and to navigate life's challenges gracefully.

I am healed—
"I will give you back your
health and heal your
wounds," says the Lord.

- Jeremiah 30:17 NLT

AWAKEN & *Reflect*

Healing isn't just about time—it's about intention, release, and transformation. As you reflect, consider how your experiences have shaped you, what you're ready to let go of, and where you're being called to grow.

AWARENESS:

What area of your life—mind, body,
or spirit—needs deeper healing?

_____

_____

_____

_____

_____

_____

_____

_____

_____

_____

_____

_____

_____

_____

_____

_____

_____

_____

WORK IT:

What is one unhealthy coping mechanism you're
ready to release? How can you replace it with
something that nurtures you?

_____

_____

_____

_____

_____

_____

_____

_____

_____

_____

_____

_____

_____

_____

_____

_____

_____

_____

ALIGNMENT:

What does true healing and wholeness look like
for you? How can you align your daily actions
with that vision?

_____

_____

_____

_____

_____

_____

_____

_____

_____

_____

_____

_____

_____

_____

_____

_____

_____

_____

_____

_____

_____

KNOWLEDGE:

What have your past struggles taught you about resilience, self-compassion, or the way your body holds onto experiences?

_____

_____

_____

_____

_____

_____

_____

_____

_____

_____

_____

_____

_____

_____

_____

_____

_____

_____

EMBRACE:

Healing is a journey, not a destination. What is one part of your healing process you are learning to accept rather than resist?

_____

_____

_____

_____

_____

_____

_____

_____

_____

_____

_____

_____

_____

_____

_____

_____

_____

_____

_____

NAVIGATE:

What is one step—big or small—you can take today to move forward in your healing journey?

_____

_____

_____

_____

_____

_____

_____

_____

_____

_____

_____

_____

_____

_____

_____

_____

_____

_____

"HE HEALS THE BROKENHEARTED AND BINDS UP THEIR WOUNDS."
— PSALM 147:3

CHAPTER ELEVEN

MINDFUL CONSUMPTION

I couldn't sleep. My mind was racing, and my throat was tight with emotion. It was barely 4:30a.m. and I found myself reaching for a joint again. I wasn't just going to lie there, battling my thoughts. I needed to smoke.

So I stepped out onto the balcony, lit up, and began to breathe in deeply—focusing on the rhythm of my inhalations. *Inhale, one... two... three... four... five... six... seven... eight.* I counted silently to myself. Then, I held my breath for four seconds before gradually exhaling as if blowing the smoke into a straw: *One... two... three... four.*

I was only half-present at first, my mind still circling around the conversation I'd had with Mike just hours earlier. He'd made a comment about my smoking being an addiction, and I couldn't help but feel defensive. *Was he right? Was that why his words stung so much?*

I could feel anger and maybe even resentment bubbling up. But then, as I continued to smoke, I noticed a shift. The anxiety began to ebb away, replaced by a calm, focused awareness. This was mindfulness in action.

I gradually worked through my emotions as I took a hit, inhaled, and exhaled. I knew Mike was right about something, though it wasn't about a weed addiction. I had told him earlier that evening that I may have had an addictive personality in the past, yes, but that wasn't the case with cannabis. The more I smoked, the more I realized that cannabis was not a crutch but a means of healing— physically, mentally, and spiritually.

I began understanding why indigenous cultures have long used plant medicine in rituals to connect with the divine. However, cannabis wasn't necessary to bring me closer to God—I'd always felt close to Him—but it did bridge the gap between my conscious mind, subconscious mind, and body.

Later, lying in bed, I struggled to breathe. My chest felt tight, my neck irritated, and the eczema behind my ears burned like fire. Panic started to rise. I couldn't get comfortable or sync my breathing with Mike's, and the irritation was overwhelming. I needed relief. Back to the balcony, I went. I accepted why I needed and wanted the plant, and I was more than okay with it. It helped me experience these feelings and deal with the discomfort of the growing and healing part.

Mike had mentioned that my eczema flare-ups might be stress-related, but what was stressing me out? My insecurities were at the forefront of my mind, and the enemy was attempting to use old thoughts to fuck with me. I was mentally, emotionally, spiritually, and physically stretched beyond my natural limits. More importantly, I wasn't numbing myself anymore. I wasn't escaping; I was facing everything head-on, armed with wisdom, strength, and a loving and understanding man by my side. As the sun rose, I made my coffee and returned to bed, feeling calmer, more centered, and ready for the new day.

Cannabis has emerged as a powerful, multifaceted tool for healing, offering wide-ranging benefits across numerous health conditions. Research shows its effectiveness in treating epilepsy; significantly reducing the frequency and intensity of seizures, particularly in patients unresponsive to traditional medications. For individuals with Crohn's disease, cannabis not only reduces inflammation and alleviates pain but, in some cases, even helps patients achieve remission. Its therapeutic potential extends to chronic conditions like multiple sclerosis, where it eases muscle spasms and stiffness, enhancing mobility and comfort. In cancer care, cannabis plays a crucial role in pain management and mitigating the side effects of chemotherapy, such as nausea and appetite loss. These diverse applications highlight cannabis's capacity to bring holistic relief, supporting both body and mind in transformative ways.

For me, cannabis has been nothing short of life-changing, helping to manage the chronic pain and inflammation caused by spinal stenosis, spondylolisthesis, osteoarthritis, bilateral carpal tunnel, and migraines. I've discovered that cannabis's versatility allows me to curate its use to my needs throughout the day, providing a natural alternative to the pharmaceuticals I once relied on.

I start my mornings with 50-100 mg of full-spectrum Loko Infused creamer in my coffee, which provides steady relief, clarity and energy until mid-morning or lunchtime. This infused creamer also helps ease my back, hip, and leg pain, allowing me to stay focused and productive. As the effects wear off, my attention span fades, my nerves feel unsettled, and the pain starts to return—at which point, I smoke my first joint.

One of the remarkable aspects of cannabis is how different strains, cannabinoids, and terpene profiles can be combined with various consumption methods to target specific symptoms. Sativa-dominant strains like Jack Herer are high in THC and known for their energizing effects, making them ideal for managing pain in the mornings. These strains contain terpenes like limonene and pinene, uplifting mood and offering anti-inflammatory benefits.

As the day progresses, I switch to balanced hybrids like Blue Dream or Kush Mints, which offer a blend of THC and CBD for both pain relief and mental clarity without excessive sedation. Their terpene profiles, rich in myrcene and caryophyllene, are particularly effective for reducing inflammation and relaxing muscles as my pain from sitting or standing too long intensifies. This combination allows me to manage my symptoms effectively while maintaining focus and energy.

In the evenings, I turn to Indica-dominant strains like Northern Lights, rich in sedative terpenes such as linalool and myrcene, which ease the day's accumulated pain and help me relax. This is particularly helpful in managing my idiopathic hypersomnia, where restful sleep is often difficult to achieve. These strains calm both my body and mind, preparing me for a more restful night.

Beyond smoking or vaping, I incorporate tinctures, topicals, concentrates, and suppositories into my routine. Tinctures provide discreet and controlled dosing, allowing me to maintain steady pain relief without the psychoactive effects of THC, helping me stay focused throughout the day.

Topicals, like CBD-infused salves and THC-rich lotions, are perfect for targeting localized pain in my neck, lower back, or legs. They also keep my skin looking vibrant and soft.

Concentrates, like vape oils and dabs, offer potent relief on days when the pain is incredibly intense or when I'm recreationally getting high with others. While I don't typically prefer vapes or dabs because the high feels different from smoking flower, I do enjoy a good dab at events from time to time. The fast-acting nature of concentrates can be a convenient option when quick relief is necessary.

I've also found significant relief from menstrual cramps and back pain through the use of CBD suppositories. These offer targeted relief with minimal psychoactive effects, allowing me to continue my day without interruption. Additionally, they can add a surprising layer of intensity to intimate moments, enhancing both pleasure and connection, making them a unique tool for managing pain and improving my overall quality of life.

In essence, cannabis has become an integral part of my daily routine, helping me navigate chronic conditions while maintaining balance and wellness. It's more than just a remedy; it's a natural, multifaceted tool that empowers me to live fully and intentionally.

Spiritually, cannabis has been a guide, deepening my introspection and connection to myself and the world around me. Through mindful consumption, I've engaged in deeper meditation and self-reflection, leading to personal growth and transformation. Cannabis has allowed me to slow down, be present, and savor the moment, helping me navigate my spiritual journey with clarity and purpose.

Mentally, cannabis has been a soothing companion

in managing anxiety, stress, and depression. THC's psychoactive effects induce relaxation, easing stress and anxiety, while CBD offers calming effects without the high, making it an effective tool for managing depression. CBN, another cannabinoid, has been particularly beneficial in addressing my sleep challenges. While research on CBN is still emerging, I have found it valuable for improving the quality of my sleep—offering a natural alternative to traditional sleep medications with fewer side effects.

Ultimately, cannabis is not a cure-all, but when used mindfully, it can be a powerful ally in the quest for healing and wholeness. Developing a thoughtful relationship with the plant has allowed me to optimize its benefits and incorporate it as part of a holistic approach to wellness. We can all find a path toward greater health and well-being by embracing the earth's natural gifts with mindfulness and intention.

"THEN GOD SAID, 'LOOK! I HAVE GIVEN YOU EVERY SEED-BEARING PLANT THROUGHOUT THE EARTH AND ALL THE FRUIT TREES FOR YOUR FOOD.'"

GENESIS 1:29 NLT

AWAKEN & *Reflect*

Healing is not just about treating symptoms—it's about being fully present with ourselves, listening to what our bodies need, and aligning with the natural rhythms of wellness. Through mindfulness, plant medicine, and intentional self-care, we create space for healing that goes beyond the physical.

AWARENESS:

Close your eyes and do a body scan. Where do you feel tension or discomfort? What emotions arise as you sit with that awareness?

_____

_____

_____

_____

_____

_____

_____

_____

_____

_____

_____

_____

_____

_____

_____

_____

_____

_____

WORK IT:

What is one belief or habit around self-care that no longer serves you? How can you replace it with a practice that truly nurtures your well-being?

_____

_____

_____

_____

_____

_____

_____

_____

_____

_____

_____

_____

_____

_____

_____

_____

_____

_____

_____

_____

_____

ALIGNMENT:

Which holistic or natural healing methods—such
as breathwork, herbal medicine, sound healing,
or meditation—help you feel more connected to
yourself? How can you integrate them into your
routine with intention?

_____

_____

_____

_____

_____

_____

_____

_____

_____

_____

_____

_____

_____

_____

_____

_____

KNOWLEDGE:

Think of a time when your body signaled a need for rest or healing. How did you respond? What did you learn from that experience?

EMBRACE:

Healing isn't just about doing—it's also about being.
How can you allow yourself more space to rest,
reflect, and receive?

_____

_____

_____

_____

_____

_____

_____

_____

_____

_____

_____

_____

_____

_____

_____

_____

_____

_____

_____

_____

NAVIGATE:

What is one mindful action—big or small—you can take today to support your healing journey, whether through movement, nourishment, or stillness?

_____

_____

_____

_____

_____

_____

_____

_____

_____

_____

_____

_____

_____

_____

_____

_____

"BE STILL, AND KNOW THAT I AM GOD."
— PSALM 46:10

CHAPTER TWELVE

I AM

Throughout the ups and downs of my life, I've learned that the search for identity can lead us down many different paths. As children, we often yearn for acceptance and love from those around us, but rejection and abandonment can leave lasting marks. We carry that pain into adulthood, seeking comfort and fulfillment in all the wrong places—whether through people, careers, vices, or fleeting successes. We often tie our identities to achievements or roles we play, yet still feel lonely, uncertain, and disconnected from our true selves.

For years, I connected my identity to my circumstances —my accomplishments, my medical conditions, and even my failures. I believed external factors like my success, parenting skills, and relationships defined my worth. However, reflecting on my journey, I realized these circumstances were merely part of a refining process. Just like gold is heated seven times to remove all impurities,

I, too, was being refined through these trials until God's reflection could be seen in me.

Each hardship was a part of this purification, whether it was a medical condition that tested my strength or a personal failure that challenged my faith. The painful moments weren't meaningless; they were a necessary part of shedding what wasn't meant for me and revealing who I truly am. God was working to burn away what didn't belong in every heated moment—the fears, doubts, and false identities I had clung to for so long.

Now, as I look back, I see that the reflection He left behind in me is one of strength, resilience, and grace. I no longer define myself by external measures but by the unwavering truth of who God says I am. I am His, and through His refining process, I have come to see my true worth and purpose.

In the Bible, Jesus uses the metaphor of darnel grass— often mistaken for wheat—to illustrate how good and bad things grow together until the harvest. Similarly, throughout my life, I encountered people and experiences that seemed valuable at first but were, in reality, distractions from my true purpose. The darnel grass, or tares, represented those elements in my life that initially appeared beneficial but ultimately hindered my growth. From the toxic relationships of high school to the traumatic times with Mr. Jones and even the complexities within my circle of friends, family, or colleagues, these deceptive influences were like impostors masquerading as genuine support. Though painful, these experiences were essential for my transformation, revealing what truly nurtures my soul and what merely obscures it.

On the other hand, the wheat represents the valuable

lessons and people that God placed in my life to help me grow and discover my true self. My connection with God was the guiding force, revealing the darnel from the wheat—the harmful from the nurturing. One example of this was my relationship with Mike. Much like Boaz, his character exudes kindness, integrity, and a deep understanding of my heart. I began to see him as an answer to prayers I had asked long before we met.

Through Mike's kindness and encouragement, I began to recognize the strength and worth God had placed within me all along. His ability to see beyond my brokenness, to lift me up when I felt most fragile, was God's way of showing me that I was not as damaged as I believed. Although I often questioned his intentions and found it difficult to trust his affirmations, I now realize that God used his presence to highlight truths planted within me long before our paths crossed.

Through Mike's quiet strength and gentle persistence, I began to understand that God had been working all along, answering my prayers in my loneliness and uncertainty. Meeting Mike was not by chance—as beautifully serendipitous as it may have seemed; it reflected God's timing and care, revealing that He had heard my cries and was shaping my journey purposefully. Even in moments of doubt, God was using Mike as a vessel to remind me of my worth, just as Boaz was to Ruth. This realization helped me begin to trust Mike's presence in my life and the deeper truth that my value had always been secure in God's eyes.

I was molded and transformed through life's hurt, habits, and hang-ups. In my deepest valleys, I discovered a profound truth: my identity isn't rooted in what I've done or what's been done to me. It's not defined by my conditions or the labels society might impose. My identity is in who God says I am.

I am not defined by abandonment, addiction, or abuse. My career, conditions, or circumstances do not define me. I am a child of God, fearfully and wonderfully made. And so are you.

This realization wasn't easy, but it has been liberating. Understanding that my identity is rooted in God's love has empowered me to let go of what no longer serves me and embrace my true self. I've come to see that God's hand has guided me through every trial and triumph, shaping me into who I was always meant to be.

Our relationship with God reveals that our true identity is already within us. We were created with a purpose, and aligning with that purpose leads us to a life of passion, joy, and fulfillment. Romans 8:37 NKJV reminds us: "In all these things we are more than conquerors through him who loved us." This isn't just a promise of victory over adversity; it's a declaration of our inherent worth and purpose.

Living out our God-given purpose means taking ownership of our thoughts, choices, and actions. We become the kings and queens of our earthly assignments by cultivating an attitude of gratitude, developing a mindset of empowerment, and equipping ourselves with the skills and tools to overcome challenges and thrive.

It's not about perfection but growth. Life is messy, and setbacks are inevitable. What matters is how we respond. As I always asked Charlotte when she was younger, "What's the difference between a good day and a bad day?"

Then I would pause and look at her as she responded with a scowl, "Your attitude."

Will we let our struggles define us, or will we rise

above them, knowing that our identity is secure in God? Embracing our worth and living in alignment with our purpose makes us unstoppable.

This understanding has fueled my passion to help others discover their identity and purpose. Through coaching, consulting, and sharing the gems I've learned, I aim to guide you toward your own awakening. My mission is to help you uncover who you truly are—not who the world says you should be, but who God created you to be.

Each of us is a masterpiece, crafted with intention and love by our Creator. Ephesians 2:10 KJV declares, "For we are God's workmanship, created in Christ Jesus to do good works, which God prepared in advance for us to do." You are not an accident. You are not here by chance. There is a divine plan for your life, and you were designed to fulfill it.

As I conclude this memoir, I want to leave you with this: No matter where you've been or what you've gone through, your story isn't over. You are not your mistakes, failures, or past. You are God's beloved. Your identity is found in Him; through Him, you can live a life of passion, purpose, and fulfillment.

May this book be the first step in your journey of awakening. I invite you to walk this path with me—to discover the fullness of who you are in God, cultivate your gifts and talents, and live a life that reflects the greatness within you.

"See, I have refined you,
though not as silver; I have
tested you in the furnace of
affliction."

Isaiah 48:10 NIV

AWAKEN & *Reflect*

Your identity is not defined by your past, your struggles, or the labels the world has placed on you. It is rooted in who God says you are—fearfully and wonderfully made, called with purpose, and deeply loved.

AWARENESS:

What limiting beliefs or labels have you allowed
to define you? How have they shaped the
way you see yourself?

_____

_____

_____

_____

_____

_____

_____

_____

_____

_____

_____

_____

_____

_____

_____

_____

_____

_____

_____

WORK IT:

What is one false identity or negative thought pattern you need to name and reframe? How can you replace it with God's truth about who you are?

_____

_____

_____

_____

_____

_____

_____

_____

_____

_____

_____

_____

_____

_____

_____

_____

_____

_____

ALIGNMENT:

What does it mean to live in alignment with your
true identity? How can you show up as the
person God created you to be?

_____

_____

_____

_____

_____

_____

_____

_____

_____

_____

_____

_____

_____

_____

_____

_____

_____

_____

_____

_____

KNOWLEDGE:

Looking back, what hardships have refined you rather than defined you? How have they shaped your understanding of yourself and your purpose?

_____

_____

_____

_____

_____

_____

_____

_____

_____

_____

_____

_____

_____

_____

_____

_____

_____

_____

EMBRACE:

What is one truth about your worth, identity, or
purpose that you are ready to fully embrace?

_____

_____

_____

_____

_____

_____

_____

_____

_____

_____

_____

_____

_____

_____

_____

_____

_____

_____

_____

_____

_____

NAVIGATE:

What is one action you can take today—whether in thought, word, or deed—that affirms your identity as a child of God?

_____

_____

_____

_____

_____

_____

_____

_____

_____

_____

_____

_____

_____

_____

_____

_____

_____

_____

"BEFORE I FORMED YOU IN THE WOMB I KNEW YOU, BEFORE YOU WERE BORN I SET YOU APART."
— JEREMIAH 1:5

JUST ASK

As you embark on your journey of self-discovery and awakening, remember that you don't have to walk this path alone. "**Ask**, and it will be given to you; **seek**, and you will find; **knock**, and the door will be opened to you." Matthew 7:7 NKJV

The Grassdoor & Co. Coaching & Consulting Services:

- Career & Life Coaching: Discover your passion and purpose and navigate life's challenges with clarity and confidence.

- Business Consulting: Turn your passion and purpose into profit and dominate your industry with tailored strategies and insights.

- Cannabis Consulting: Explore plant medicine and alternative healing modalities to support your mind, body, and spirit.

- Referrals & Resources: Connect with experts in trauma healing, holistic wellness, financial literacy, estate planning, advocacy, and more!

To get started, reach out directly or scan the QR code below.

Let's grow & thrive together! Reach out today and take the first step toward your awakening!

Recommended Reading

Boundaries: When to Say Yes, How to Say No to Take Control of Your Life

  • Authors: Dr. Henry Cloud and Dr. John Townsend

The Body Keeps the Score: Brain, Mind, and Body in the Healing of Trauma

  • Author: Dr. Bessel van der Kolk

When the Body Says No: The Cost of Hidden Stress

  • Author: Dr. Gabor Maté

Digital Resource:

  • YouVersion Bible App

  • Description: A free, comprehensive Bible app offering various versions, reading plans, and audio options.

  • Access: https://www.bible.com/app

Acknowledgments

To Giovanni, thank you for having my back, always. Thank you for being a loving and fun uncle, a supportive brother, and a solid business partner. Lastly, thank you for driving me everywhere. I love and appreciate you, Brother.

To my mom, thank you for helping me become the woman I am today. Thank you for doing your best and supporting me when needed. Lastly, thank you for letting Charlotte stay at your house for an entire week so I could complete this book.

To Baba, thank you for the life lessons and for helping me realize how much I appreciate mindfulness—simply smoking outdoors, nice vibes, and a good cup of coffee.

To Uncle Michael, thank you for *The Greatest Love of All*, your regular check-ins, and for inspiring the vision behind this book cover.

To David, thank you for being a real day one, always willing to come to my rescue, being an amazing Godfather to Charlotte, and, of course, for sending your daily memes.

To Jhanelle GF, no matter how often we talk or see each other, it's like we never skip a beat. Your support and creativity helped bring this book—and its cover—to life. Thank you for always showing up in the ways that matter most.

To Sonia, you honestly feel like my professional OG confidante. You have guided and supported me for nearly seven years, especially as I walked through some of my darkest valleys. I would not have become the person I needed to be to write this book without you. You led me to discover love, peace, joy, and healing. Thank you for your authenticity, Godly counsel, and especially for believing in me and being proud when I couldn't provide that for myself.

Lastly, **to my Kickstarter Backers**, thank you for believing in me, this book, and the awakening movement it represents. Your support is more than a contribution—it's a declaration that healing, truth, and transformation matter. This wouldn't be possible without your generosity, faith, and shared vision. You are forever part of this journey.

About the Author

Aisa Marie Magsombol is a serial entrepreneur, author, and advocate whose journey inspires those who have faced adversity. As a career and life coach, business consultant, and recruitment strategist, she brings a unique perspective to personal and professional transformation. Aisa is the founder of The Grassdoor & Co., HauteMonde Furniture, and co-founder of Top Shelf Social, demonstrating her expertise in turning vision into reality.

Beyond her business ventures, Aisa is deeply committed to advocacy. She works with organizations such as the Hypersomnia Foundation, EveryLife Foundation for Rare Diseases, Rare Across America, and the Rare Compassion Program, raising awareness and empowering others to use their voices for change. As a guest speaker for Reaching Every Patient: A Health Equity Conversation, she passionately advocates for health equity and access to care, particularly within the rare disease community.

Aisa's entrepreneurial spirit has also led her to share insights as a Cannapreneur on The CryptoCannaverse Show and as a contributor to Forbes Councils' Conversations Amongst Entrepreneurs, discussing the intersection of women, business, and mental health.

In *Awaken*, Aisa offers readers a transformative journey of self-reflection, self-discovery, and spirituality. Her memoir is a powerful testament that, with faith and resilience, we can move from survival to revival.

Connect with Aisa:

✉ aisamarie@thegrassdoornco.com

☎ 909.480.1420

◎ Instagram: @thegrassdoornco_
                @aisamariewrites

in www.linkedin.com/in/aisamarie

◉ www.thegrassdoornco.com